THE NEW CLARENDON SHAKESPEARE

AS YOU LIKE IT

Edited by

ISABEL J. BISSON
Formerly Lecturer in English
in the University of
Birmingham

OXFORD UNIVERSITY PRESS

Oxford University Press, Walton Street, Oxford OX2 6DP

OXFORD NEW YORK TORONTO
DELHI BOMBAY CALCUTTA MADRAS KARACHI
PETALING JAYA SINGAPORE HONG KONG TOKYO
NAIROBI DAR ES SALAAM CAPE TOWN
MELBOURNE AUCKLAND

and associated companies in
BERLIN IBADAN

Oxford is a trade mark of Oxford University Press

First published 1941
Reprinted 1943, 1946, 1947, 1951, 1953, 1955,
1960, 1964, 1966, 1971, 1973, 1975, 1978, 1980, 1985
1989

THE NEW CLARENDON SHAKESPEARE

Under the general editorship of R. E. C. HOUGHTON, M.A.

	Edited by
Antony and Cleopatra	R. E. C. Houghton
As You Like It	Isabel J. Bisson
Coriolanus	B. H. Kemball-Cook
Hamlet	George Rylands
Henry IV, Part I	Bertram Newman
Henry IV, Part II	William R. Rutland
Henry V	Ronald F. W. Fletcher
Julius Caesar	R. E. C. Houghton
King Lear	R. E. C. Houghton
Macbeth	Bernard Groom
Measure for Measure	R. E. C. Houghton
Merchant of Venice	Ronald F. W. Fletcher
Midsummer Night's Dream	F. C. Horwood
Much Ado about Nothing	Philip Wayne
Othello	F. C. Horwood and R. E. C. Houghton
Richard II	John M. Lothian
Richard III	R. E. C. Houghton
Romeo and Juliet	R. E. C. Houghton
The Tempest	J. R. Sutherland
The Winter's Tale	S. L. Bethell
Twelfth Night	J. C. Dent

Printed in Hong Kong

GENERAL PREFACE

THIS edition of Shakespeare aims primarily at presenting the text in such a way that it can be easily read and understood. The language of Shakespeare presents considerable difficulties to the beginner, difficulties which are soon forgotten and overlooked by readers who are familiar with the plays. The answers of examination candidates often reveal unexpected ignorance of quite ordinary Shakespearian phraseology and vocabulary. In the notes, therefore, the main emphasis has been placed on the interpretation of words and phrases. Textual and linguistic matter, to which much space was given in the old Clarendon Press editions of Wright and Clark, has been kept in the background, but explanation is prominent. The notes have been divided; words and phrases capable of a short explanation are glossed at the foot of the page, while the more difficult passages are treated after the text in the general commentary.

In the commentary alternative explanations and the mention of critics by name have been avoided as far as possible; on the other hand there are a number of less elementary notes on textual points and other matters not strictly necessary for younger students, and these appear in smaller type and within square brackets.

After the commentary is printed a substantial selection from the best criticism of the play, old and new; a feature in which this edition of Shakespeare follows the plan set by the Clarendon English series. Here some matter will be found suitable for more advanced students; and the inclusion of varying opinions will provide material for reflection and comparison. It is the editor's belief that students can best be taught to criticize by the provision of material which they may use as a starting-point as well as a model,

ACKNOWLEDGEMENTS

ACKNOWLEDGEMENT is gratefully made to the following for permission to reprint passages from copyright works: Dr. A. A. Jack (Unpublished Lecture Notes); Sir Edmund Chambers and Messrs. Blackie & Son, Ltd. (Preface to *As You Like It* in the Red Letter Shakespeare); Miss Evelyn Brooke and Messrs. Constable & Co., Ltd. (Rev. Stopford Brooke, *On Ten Plays of Shakespeare*); Messrs. Kegan Paul, Trench, Trubner & Co., Ltd. (Edward Dowden, *Shakespeare: His Mind and Art*); Mr. John Masefield and Messrs. Thornton Butterworth, Ltd. (*Shakespeare*); Mr. J. B. Priestley and John Lane the Bodley Head, Ltd. (*English Comic Characters*).

The text of As You Like It *here printed is free from omission or alteration.*

CONTENTS

INTRODUCTION 7
   Date of Composition 7
   Sources of the Play 9
   Text of the Play 11
   The Plot of the Play 13
   The Play on the Shakespearian Stage . . . 16
   Note on Dramatis Personae 18

AS YOU LIKE IT 21

NOTES 119

SELECT LITERARY CRITICISM
   The Play in General 159
   The Mood of the Play 162
   The Play in Shakespeare's Development . . 162
   The Love Theme in the Play 166
   The Character of Rosalind 168
   The Character of Jaques 169
   The Character of Touchstone 172

APPENDIXES
   I. Life of William Shakespeare with a Table of his Plays 176
   II. A Note on Shakespeare's Language . . . 178
   III. A Note on Metre 185
   IV. Summary of Lodge's *Rosalynde* . . . 187

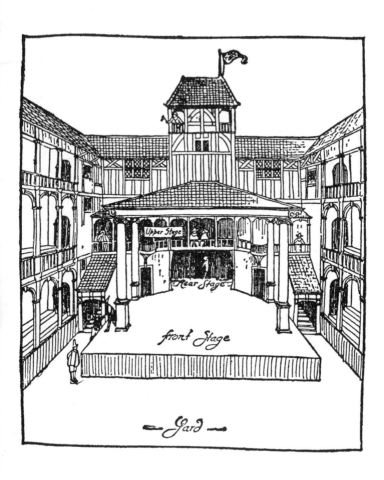

INTRODUCTION

As You Like It was written shortly before *Twelfth Night* in the period when Shakespeare's genius in romantic comedy attained its ripest maturity. When it is set beside *Twelfth Night*, the rather later play is clearly seen to have the fuller poetry and the lovelier music, the fresher zest and spirit, the richer, more varied comedy. But then *Twelfth Night* is the finest writing of its kind anywhere. In England, at least, *As You Like It* is only less of a favourite; and, after a period of neglect, since 1740 it has never been long off the stage. The unreal action alternately lags and hurries; but, as Hazlitt said, it is the 'most ideal' of Shakespeare's comedies, and 'it is not what is done, but what is said' that matters. Touchstone is the first of Shakespeare's great Fools, whose wit illumines the particular action of the play and the whole business of life; and, in addition, there is the 'melancholy' of Jaques and the spirit, tenderness, and fun of Rosalind—a perennial delight, and a challenge to which few actresses are equal. The tone of this comedy, perhaps the mood in which it was written, is a little tired, but it is mellow and serene; and *As You Like It* has another beauty, a pervasive poetry more easily felt in England than abroad. To his fellow countrymen, as to Shakespeare himself, Arden is their native woodland.

DATE OF COMPOSITION

The first mention we have of *As You Like It* is a note in the Stationers' Register, under the date 4 August 1600, directing four plays belonging to Shakespeare's company, the Lord Chancellor's Men, 'to be staied'. These four plays are *As You Like It*, *Henry the Fifth*, *Every Man in his Humour*, *Much Ado about Nothing*. The meaning of the 'staying' is that permission to publish had been sought by a printer who hoped to make money out of their popularity on the stage by issuing a text of the plays which he had, somehow, procured; and the Lord Chancellor's Men, or Shakespeare himself, intervened to prevent this piratical publication. Three of the four—*Henry the Fifth, Every Man in his Humour, Much Ado about Nothing*—were printed in the same year, all three, probably, with the consent of the actors' company to which they belonged. But, so far as is known, no Quarto of *As You Like It* ever appeared; when published in the First Folio of 1623 it is mentioned among the plays not hitherto printed.

The staying Order, then, serves to show that *As You Like It* was a popular play on the stage by 4 August 1600. Though Francis Meres, in his *Palladis Tamia*, does not purport to give a full list of Shakespeare's writings up to date (7 September 1598), the fact that he does not mention *As You Like It* suggests that he did not know it, and he was certain to know a popular play. This negative evidence that it did not exist in the autumn of 1598 is strengthened by a small piece of internal evidence. In III. v. 81, Phebe quotes a line from Marlowe's *Hero and Leander*, which was not printed till shortly after it was entered in the Stationers' Register for 2 March 1598, though Marlowe had died in 1593. There is nothing to prove that Shakespeare had not read the poem in manuscript either before Marlowe's death or at some time in the intervening years; but a reference to it on the stage, the direct quotation of a line and the mention of its author, the implication that it is known to the audience as well as to Phebe, and known to be Marlowe's— these suggest that Shakespeare quoted it in his play at a time when the poem was fresh, but established, in people's minds: i.e. after, but not very long after, its publication.

There is no clear evidence, either external or internal, to fix the date of composition more closely in the two years from September 1598 to August 1600; but a consensus of opinion puts it late rather than early within those limits. Evidence of style, metre, and general tone and handling help to indicate late 1599 or the first part of 1600. The real disagreement is on whether *As You Like It* was then composed or revised. From the date of Lodge's *Rosalynde* (1590), from various contemporary references, especially one to the death of Marlowe in 1593 (III. iii. 11–12, and note), and from certain signs of hasty alteration, it has been argued by some critics that the play, as we have it, is a rapid revision, in 1599–1600, of a draft, or even play, written in 1593–4. For the existence of this earlier draft or play no external evidence whatsoever has been found.

If, however, the play *may* have had a growing life before 4 August 1600, it almost certainly had one after that date. In the twenty-three years that intervened before its publication, it underwent some change in the theatre, in course of being acted. The Masque of Hymen, especially, and its immediate context do not look like the un-contaminated work of Shakespeare (see notes to v. iv. 104 and 144). But most authorities, however they differ in detail, agree that *As You Like It*, much as we know it, was composed at the turn of the century, and was the immediate forerunner of *Twelfth Night*.

SOURCES OF THE PLAY

Shakespeare took the title of his play from a phrase in the *Address to the Gentlemen Readers* prefixed to a novel by Thomas Lodge (1558–1625), called *Rosalynde*; Lodge's 'If you like it, so' becomes 'As you like it'.

From this novel, published in 1590, he took much more than a hint for a whimsical title, for it gave him the main characters and the outline of his story. Behind *Rosalynde*, however, lies another source, for Lodge if not for Shake-speare; and that is the fourteenth-century *Tale of Gamelyn*,

which, because it was preserved in manuscripts of the
Canterbury Tales, has sometimes been wrongly attributed
to Chaucer. Though not printed till 1721, *Gamelyn* was
accessible to Lodge in manuscript. There he found the
story of the dead nobleman with three sons; the will whose
terms induce the eldest, John, to ill-treat the youngest,
Gamelyn; the wrestling-match; the faithful servant, Adam
the Spencer; and their escape to join a band of outlaws of
whom Gamelyn becomes the captain. In the end, he serves
rough justice on all his enemies and finishes by being made
Chief Justice, and living to a ripe, healthy, and wealthy age.
Small coincidences of detail between *As You Like It* and
the *Tale of Gamelyn*, especially where the play and the
poem agree against the novel, have convinced some critics
that Shakespeare knew and was following the poem. But
the similarities are probably accidental, and the matter is
of little importance, were it not for what it might tell us,
indirectly, of Shakespeare's acquaintance with Chaucer's
genuine poems.

   To the framework of *Gamelyn*, Lodge added a pastoral
setting and a sentimental, artificial vein of feeling and
speech much in fashion at the time. He also introduced
the situation of the usurper, Torismond (Frederick), and
his banished brother, Gerismond (Duke Senior), who in
Lodge is a King of France; and from the wrestling-match
onwards he developed a love theme or rather several love
themes which completely change the course of the *Gamelyn*
story. Adam the Spencer, John = Saladyne, Gamelyn
= Rosader remain; but Rosalynde-Ganimede (Rosalind),
Alinda-Aliena (Celia), Montanus (Silvius), Phoebe, and
Coridon (Corin) make their appearance. There is no
question whatever of the extent of Shakespeare's debt to
Lodge, for with minor differences in action and incident
the course of his novel is that of *As You Like It* (see
Appendix IV).

But to Lodge's story Shakespeare in turn made additions. It was he who imagined Touchstone and Jaques, and, though Lodge has flashes of insight and portraiture, gave the other characters a life immeasurably more full and real than their pleasantly conventional existence in his original.

Two minor debts have been, by some, suspected. The first is to Drayton's *Polyolbion*, a rimed and sometimes poetic description of England, on which, according to Francis Meres, he was already at work in 1598, though the first 18 Books only appeared in 1612. But there is no evidence that it was written before *As You Like It*; and Furness is undoubtedly right in thinking that the impression left by the poem, especially the elaborated picture of the hermit, is that Drayton described Arden with *As You Like It* affectionately in mind.

The second suggested source for a small part of the play (III. ii. 1–8, and Orlando's verses generally) is the *Orlando Furioso* of Robert Greene. This play was being acted about 1592; and in it an enemy of Orlando tries to make him jealous by carving his lady's name on the bark of trees and hanging poems celebrating her on their boughs. But a lover carving love-poems on the bark of trees was in Lodge before it was in either Greene or Shakespeare, and in fact the passage in *As You Like It* is very like the parallel passage in *Rosalynde*.

THE TEXT OF THE PLAY

The text of *As You Like It* offers few difficulties, for the First Folio of 1623 is our only authority. Probably taken from a copy in use in the theatre (see notes to I. ii. 196; v. iv. 104), it is, fortunately, a good text. Most of its corruptions are due merely to faulty proof-reading, some of them corrected by the compositor of the Second Folio (e.g. II. iii. 58; IV. iii. 155, and notes); of the remaining ones there are few that seriously affect the sense (see notes to I. ii. 151; II. iv. 1; II. vii. 54–5; II. vii. 73; IV. i. 18; V. ii. 91–3).

It was in reference to a word in this play that Dr. Johnson laid down a golden rule for dealing with the Quarto and Folio versions of Shakespeare's text: 'elegance alone will not justify alteration' (see note to II. vii. 95). In this edition, therefore, the text of the First Folio has been closely followed, even to the extent of rejecting certain emendations which Johnson himself was prepared to accept (e.g. see note to I. ii. 129). None have been included in this text unless they seemed strictly necessary, and they are recorded in the notes (e.g. I. ii. 76; I. ii. 257; II. vii. 54–5; IV. iii. 155; V. iii. 29). The silent deviations from the Folio are confined to the correction of punctuation and obvious misprints, and the amplifying of the stage directions. In both particulars, as indeed in the text generally, the Oxford edition has been closely adhered to, except, here and there, in punctuation and in the rejection of emendations. Interesting examples of the latter will be found in II. i. 5; II. i. 18; III. ii. 153; IV. i. 96, where, for reasons discussed in the notes, the Folio readings have been kept; all other deviations from the Oxford text are recorded below. The result is a conservative but, the editor believes, an intelligible text of *As You Like It*.

[The present edition follows the text of the Oxford Shakespeare with the following exceptions. The readings of F. are restored in: I. i. 41 ('him' for 'he'); I. ii. 129 ('see' for 'feel'); I. ii. 151 ('princess calls' for 'princes call'); I. ii. 250 ('misconsters' for 'misconstrues'); II. i. 5 ('not' for 'but'); II. i. 18 ('I would not change it' given to Amiens instead of the Duke); II. iii. 8 ('bonny' for 'bony'); II. iv. 34 ('in' for 'with'); II. v. 16 (''em' for 'them'); II. vii. 23 ('may' and 'we' transposed); III. i. 1 ('see' for 'seen'); III. ii. 153 ('Jupiter' for 'pulpiter'); III. ii. 252 ('buy' for 'be wi''); III. v. 66 ('your' for 'her'); IV. i. 18 ('in' inserted; 'my' for 'by'); IV. i. 29 ('buy' for 'be wi''); IV. i. 96 ('chroniclers' for 'coroners'); IV. i. 145

('had' for 'hath'); IV. iii. 3 ('a' deleted); IV. iii. 33 ('women's' for 'woman's'); IV. iii. 87 ('but' deleted); V. iv. 11 ('that' deleted); V. iv. 21 ('you' inserted); V. iv. 111 ('his' for 'her'); V. iv. 183 ('deserves' for 'deserve'). The punctuation has also been altered in: I. i. 3; I. ii. 69–70; I. ii. 77; I. iii. 82; II. i. 5–6; II. i. 22; III. ii. 36; III. v. 17; IV. i. 18; IV. i. 97; IV. iii. 75.]

THE PLOT OF THE PLAY

I. i. Orlando, the youngest son of Sir Rowland de Boys, complains to Adam, an old family servant, that his eldest brother ignores the terms of his dead father's will, by which Oliver, the heir, was to maintain him as befitted his birth. After a violent quarrel, Oliver incites a professional wrestler to punish Orlando in a match that is to take place the following day.

I. ii. Rosalind, daughter of a banished Duke, and Celia, daughter of his usurping brother, are deeply attached to one another. Their chief amusement at Court is jesting with the Fool, Touchstone, and the three tease an affected nobleman who comes to tell them of the wrestling match, which takes place in their presence. Both princesses feel pity for the youthful Orlando, and between Rosalind and Orlando it is love at first sight. He defeats the wrestler; but is warned to leave the Court at once because the Duke and his father had been enemies.

I. iii. The Duke, who has begun to nurse suspicions of his niece, angrily dismisses Rosalind from his Court. Celia insists that she will go with her, and the two plan their escape to Rosalind's father in the Forest of Arden. Celia is to go as a girl, Aliena, Rosalind disguised as a gallant boy, Ganymede, and they take Touchstone with them for company.

II. i. Rosalind's father, Duke Senior, and his followers in Arden talk contentedly about the advantages of their simple life, and about an absent comrade, Jaques, whose moralizing habits of mind and speech amuse the exiles.

II. ii. The usurping Duke discovers his daughter's flight with her cousin, and, hearing that Orlando may be with them, sends to seek him, or, failing him, his brother Oliver.

II. iii. Adam warns Orlando to flee, because Oliver means that night to burn his lodging over his head. Old Adam offers the penniless Orlando the money he has saved from his wages, imploring him to take him with him in his flight.

II. iv. Rosalind, Celia, and Touchstone, very weary, at last reach the Forest of Arden, and there overhear a young shepherd confess his love-sorrows to an old one, Corin. The old man offers them shelter in his humble cottage.

II. v. Amiens, one of the banished Duke's followers, sings a song at the request of Jaques, who sourly parodies the song in a cynical stanza.

II. vi. Orlando and Adam reach Arden, Adam fainting with hunger. Orlando leaves him to seek food.

II. vii. Duke Senior and his lords are seated at table eating when Jaques comes to tell them of his meeting with Touchstone in the Forest. Orlando rushes in with sword drawn, demanding food. The Duke sends him to fetch Adam, and, learning that he is the son of an old friend, makes him welcome to his band.

III. i. The usurping Duke orders Oliver to find Orlando within a year, seizing all his possessions until he does so.

III. ii. Touchstone is jesting with Corin about a shepherd's life when Rosalind joins them, reading a poem in her praise which she has found in the Forest. Celia comes to them reading another, and reveals that the writer is Orlando, of whom she has caught sight. The two girls hide as Orlando and Jaques approach, and, when Jaques leaves him, Rosalind and Orlando have a long talk in which she maintains her boyish character. He agrees to play a game with her by which she undertakes to cure him of his love-sickness if he will always treat her, not as Ganymede, but as his beloved Rosalind.

III. iii. Touchstone woos a stupid country girl, Audrey, with Jaques as an amused witness. On the point of being married to her he changes his mind for the moment.

III. iv. Orlando is late for an appointment with Rosalind, whom Celia teases about her lover's want of fidelity. Corin summons them to go with him to see a meeting between Silvius and Phebe.

III. v. They hear Phebe's disdainful treatment of her suitor, and Rosalind takes her sharply to task for her pride. Phebe falls deeply in love with Ganymede (Rosalind), and makes Silvius promise to be the bearer of a letter in which she will answer Rosalind's scorn with scorn.

IV. i. Rosalind is discussing Jaques' 'melancholy' with him when Orlando approaches. She at first ignores him in punishment for his lateness, but soon they are deep in talk about love—Orlando pretending that Ganymede is his Rosalind. He promises to return to her in two hours.

IV. ii. Jaques meets the Duke's lords on their way back from hunting, and they sing a round as they go.

IV. iii. Rosalind and Celia are waiting for Orlando, who is again late, when Silvius brings Phebe's letter, which Rosalind reads aloud. Silvius is dumbfounded to learn that it is a letter of love, not of scorn; but his passion for Phebe is incurable, and he returns to her. Oliver brings Rosalind a handkerchief stained with Orlando's blood, and explains how his brother has been wounded in rescuing him from a lioness. Rosalind faints on receiving the token, though she insists that her faint is only pretence.

V. i. Audrey is reproaching Touchstone for breaking off their marriage when a former rustic lover of hers joins them, only to be wittily dismissed by Touchstone.

V. ii. Oliver tells Orlando that he and Celia have fallen

in love at first sight, and goes off to prepare her for their marriage on the morrow. Rosalind finds Orlando sad at the contrast between his brother's happiness and his own longing for her. She promises to make him, Silvius, and Phebe completely happy at the wedding next day.

V. iii. Touchstone and Audrey, also, are planning to be married the following day when they meet two of the Duke's pages who sing a song.

V. iv. Rosalind declares to the assembled company that she will solve the lovers' difficulties, and leaves them while Touchstone entertains them by a display of his wit. A masque follows in which Hymen presents his daughter (no longer disguised) to the Duke, and joins the several pairs of lovers. News is brought that the usurping Duke has been converted, joined a religious order, and handed back his dukedom to Duke Senior and their lands to his exiled followers. Jaques decides to throw in his lot with the convert, and leaves the happy company to their revelry.

The play ends with an Epilogue spoken by Rosalind.

THE PLAY ON THE SHAKESPEARIAN STAGE

The Elizabethan theatre was a very different affair from the modern one. The latter, a 'picture stage' in which the audience may be said to constitute the 'fourth wall' of a room, aims at illusion; the former, in which the stage was a platform thrust out among an audience, could not hope for this. A glance at the illustration will make a long explanation unnecessary. The platform constitutes the front or main stage; entrance was at the back (through any of several doors), not at the sides, so that some time elapsed between a character's appearance and his reaching the front of the stage. The building at the rear had a gallery above, which served for walls of a city, balcony of a room, &c. Below were curtains which, when drawn back, served to provide a *rear* or *inner stage*. As there was no means of closing the outer stage, scenes which had to be disclosed or hidden took place on this inner stage. There was little approximation to scenery, but plenty of movable properties (e.g. a 'mossy bank').

A phrase in *As You Like It*—'this wide and universal theatre' (II. vii. 137, and note)—is generally taken to refer to the Globe Theatre, which was completed in 1599, and in which most of Shakespeare's plays were subsequently acted. It therefore gives an interesting hint of the stage and auditorium which he had in mind in writing *As You Like It*; they cannot have been very different from those of the theatre in the illustration on page 6, which was being built a couple of years later. Most of the action of the play must have taken place on the outer stage. In the first scene the quarrel of the two brothers would be acted there; in the second, the spectacle of the wrestling-match, again, must have been near the front of the outer stage, with the crowd grouped at the sides, and the Duke, Rosalind, Celia, and their immediate attendants withdrawn to watch from a more privileged position just within the recess. Similarly, both recess and outer stage were probably used in the third scene. In the absence of a drop-curtain, the swift succession of scenes in Acts II and III, with their alternation between the Court and Arden, was managed by a skilful use of the curtained recess. To indicate meetings in various parts of the forest, it was sufficient for characters to come on the stage from a side different from that used for the *exit* from the previous scene; but for the short Court scenes in these two acts the curtains would be opened and the recess used, the action returning to Arden on the outer stage. The recess, however, must also have been used for some of the Arden scenes, those where Duke Senior is discovered talking with his followers, probably in II. i, and certainly in II. vii; and it may have been used for II. v, where Amiens sings to his comrades, the outer stage being kept to represent the long scenes in the open forest. So, also, throughout Acts IV and V, though in v. iv, the important lookers-on at the Masque of Hymen probably withdrew into the recess, as on the occasion of the wrestling-match. The play gives no opportunity for using the gallery.

At one point the Elizabethan producer of *As You Like It* was faced with a real difficulty in the absence of a drop-curtain. At the close of Act II. vi, Orlando leaves Adam, fainting, and rushes off to find food; in the next scene he has to break in on the Duke and his lords, be sent to fetch Adam, and return to them carrying the old man. Orlando would leave Adam lying at the side of the outer stage, in full view of the audience, go out, rush in from the other entrance to find the Duke and his lords at table in the recess, go out again, pick up Adam and carry him to the Duke's table. If this seems to us cruder than our modern practice, we must remember that the Elizabethan expected none of that illusion of reality to which we are accustomed, and instinctively accepted the stage conventions in which he had grown up.

The play is particularly rich in hints of the imagined scenery which did not exist on the Elizabethan stage. It would be interesting to know whether it was ever acted in the open air, as it often is to-day, in a setting to suggest Arden.

NOTE ON DRAMATIS PERSONAE

Duke Senior. He is only so-called in Folio Stage Directions, and the adjective explains itself.

Duke Frederick. The choice of his name was so hap-hazard that Shakespeare in one instance may even have forgotten for the moment what it was; see I. ii. 76–7, note.

Jaques. The name was fairly common as a surname in Warwickshire in and before Shakespeare's time. The question of its pronunciation is discussed in II. i. 26, note. The word 'jakes' meant a privy, and it is possible that Shakespeare is hinting at this in using the name for a character who had been a 'libertine' (see II. vii. 64–9). At any rate, the name should be thought of as English, having nothing to do here with French Jacques<Jacobus.

Orlando. Sir John Harington's translation (1591) of Ariosto's poem *Orlando Furioso* familiarized the name as that of a lover-hero; and it may have been further suggested to Shakespeare by Greene's play with the same title, based on this translation (see *ante*, Sources of the Play).

Rosalind (Ganymede), Aliena, Adam, Phebe are all taken from Lodge.

Celia appears to be chosen in preference to Lodge's less musical Alinda, like *Oliver* for Saladyne.

Corin and *Silvius* are typical names in pastoral literature; *William* and *Audrey* are Elizabethan rustic names that would naturally suggest themselves.

Touchstone is an invented name which may suggest that his wit acts as a 'touchstone' for other men's wisdom. But any unlikely name would do for a Fool; in *Lear* Shakespeare leaves the greatest of his Fools nameless.

Sir Oliver Martext. Martext would be a suitable comic name for a village clergyman, but Jaques and Touchstone both suggest (III. iii. 59–97) that this priest is not regularly ordained, and his name may be inspired by the Puritan 'Marprelate' controversy of the early nineties. *Sir* is simply the Elizabethan title for the Latin Dominus: one who has taken his degree at the University, cf. Scots, 'dominie' for a graduate schoolmaster.

DRAMATIS PERSONÆ

DUKE, living in exile.
FREDERICK, his Brother, Usurper of his Dominions.
AMIENS, } Lords attending upon the banished Duke.
JAQUES, }
LE BEAU, a Courtier, attending upon Frederick.
CHARLES, a Wrestler.
OLIVER, }
JAQUES, } Sons of Sir Rowland de Boys.
ORLANDO, }
ADAM, } Servants to Oliver.
DENNIS, }
TOUCHSTONE, a Clown.
SIR OLIVER MARTEXT, a Vicar.
CORIN, } Shepherds.
SILVIUS, }
WILLIAM, a Country Fellow, in love with Audrey.
A person representing Hymen.

ROSALIND, Daughter to the banished Duke.
CELIA, Daughter to Frederick.
PHEBE, a Shepherdess.
AUDREY, a Country Wench.

    Lords, Pages, Foresters, and Attendants.

SCENE.—*First,* OLIVER'S *Orchard near his House; afterwards, in the Usurper's Court, and in the Forest of Arden.*

AS YOU LIKE IT

ACT I

Scene I. An Orchard near Oliver's House

Enter ORLANDO *and* ADAM.

Orlando. As I remember, Adam, it was upon this
fashion bequeathed me by will but poor a thousand
crowns, and, as thou sayest, charged my brother, on
his blessing, to breed me well: and there begins my
sadness. My brother Jaques he keeps at school, and   5
report speaks goldenly of his profit: for my part, he
keeps me rustically at home, or, to speak more
properly, stays me here at home unkept; for call you
that keeping for a gentleman of my birth, that differs
not from the stalling of an ox? His horses are bred   10
better; for, besides that they are fair with their feeding, they are taught their manage, and to that end
riders dearly hired: but I, his brother, gain nothing
under him but growth, for the which his animals on his
dunghills are as much bound to him as I. Besides this   15
nothing that he so plentifully gives me, the something
that nature gave me, his countenance seems to take
from me: he lets me feed with his hinds, bars me the

*Glossarial notes dealing with words and phrases, and paraphrases of
difficult passages, are given at the foot of the page where such seem
necessary to keep the sense running. Other notes are printed in the
commentary at the end. The sign [N] in the footnotes indicates that a
further note on the same line will be found in the commentary.*

5 **school**: University [N].   8 **stays me . . . unkept**: detains
me . . . not properly supported.   12 **manage**: paces of a trained
horse (Fr. *manège*).   15 **bound**: beholden, in debt.   17 **his
countenance**: his treatment, style of living which he allows me.
18 **hinds**: menials.

place of a brother, and, as much as in him lies, mines
my gentility with my education. This is it, Adam,   20
that grieves me; and the spirit of my father, which I
think is within me, begins to mutiny against this servi-
tude. I will no longer endure it, though yet I know no
wise remedy how to avoid it.

Adam. Yonder comes my master, your brother.   25

Orlando. Go apart, Adam, and thou shalt hear how he
will shake me up.

Enter OLIVER.

Oliver. Now, sir! what make you here?

Orlando. Nothing: I am not taught to make anything.

Oliver. What mar you then, sir?   30

Orlando. Marry, sir, I am helping you to mar that which
God made, a poor unworthy brother of yours, with idleness.

Oliver. Marry, sir, be better employed, and be naught
awhile.   34

Orlando. Shall I keep your hogs, and eat husks with
them? What prodigal portion have I spent, that I should
come to such penury?

Oliver. Know you where you are, sir?

Orlando. O! sir, very well: here in your orchard.

Oliver. Know you before whom, sir?   40

Orlando. Ay, better than him I am before knows me.
I know you are my eldest brother; and, in the gentle
condition of blood, you should so know me. The
courtesy of nations allows you my better, in that you
are the first-born; but the same tradition takes not   45
away my blood, were there twenty brothers betwixt
us. I have as much of my father in me as you; albeit,

19–20 **mines my gentility**: undermines my gentle birth.   27
shake me up: abuse me roughly.   28 **make you**: are you doing.
33 **be naught**: a mischief on you! shut up!   36 **prodigal**:
extravagant [*N*].   42–3 **in the gentle condition of blood**:
according to the custom of men who are well-born.

I confess, your coming before me is nearer to his reverence.

Oliver. What, boy!   50

Orlando. Come, come, elder brother, you are too young in this.

Oliver. Wilt thou lay hands on me, villain?

Orlando. I am no villain; I am the youngest son of Sir Rowland de Boys; he was my father, and he is   55 thrice a villain that says such a father begot villains. Wert thou not my brother, I would not take this hand from thy throat till this other had pulled out thy tongue for saying so: thou hast railed on thyself.

Adam. [*Coming forward.*] Sweet masters, be patient: for your father's remembrance, be at accord.   61

Oliver. Let me go, I say.

Orlando. I will not, till I please: you shall hear me. My father charged you in his will to give me good education: you have trained me like a peasant,   65 obscuring and hiding from me all gentleman-like qualities. The spirit of my father grows strong in me, and I will no longer endure it; therefore allow me such exercises as may become a gentleman, or give me the poor allottery my father left me by testament; with   70 that I will go buy my fortunes.

Oliver. And what wilt thou do? beg, when that is spent? Well, sir, get you in: I will not long be troubled with you; you shall have some part of your will: I pray you, leave me.   75

Orlando. I will no further offend you than becomes me for my good.

48–9 **your . . . reverence**: being older you have inherited a greater share of his importance and respected position.   51 **young**: inexperienced [*N*].   53 **villain**: low-born fellow (O.Fr. *vilein*). 59 **railed on thyself**: attacked your own birth.   69 **exercises**: occupations.   70 **allottery**: portion.

Oliver. Get you with him, you old dog.

Adam. Is 'old dog' my reward? Most true, I have lost my teeth in your service. God be with my old master! he would not have spoke such a word.   81

> [*Exeunt* ORLANDO *and* ADAM.

Oliver. Is it even so? begin you to grow upon me? I will physic your rankness, and yet give no thousand crowns neither. Holla, Dennis!

Enter DENNIS.

Dennis. Calls your worship? *?. what does it mean*   85

Oliver. Was not Charles the duke's wrestler here to speak with me?

Dennis. So please you, he is here at the door, and importunes access to you.

Oliver. Call him in. [*Exit* DENNIS.] 'Twill be a good way; and to-morrow the wrestling is.   91

Enter CHARLES.

Charles. Good morrow to your worship.

Oliver. Good Monsieur Charles, what's the new news at the new court?

Charles. There's no news at the court, sir, but the   95
old news: that is, the old duke is banished by his
younger brother the new duke; and three or four
loving lords have put themselves into voluntary exile
with him, whose lands and revenues enrich the new
duke; therefore he gives them good leave to wander.   100

Oliver. Can you tell if Rosalind, the duke's daughter, be banished with her father?

---

82 **begin you . . . me**: are you beginning to grow up and hence encroach on me and give me trouble?   83 **physic your rankness**: give you something to cure this excessive growth which produces such insolence.   100 **good leave**: permission willingly granted.

Charles. O, no; for the duke's daughter, her cousin, so loves her,—being ever from their cradles bred together,—that she would have followed her exile, or 105 have died to stay behind her. She is at the court, and no less beloved of her uncle than his own daughter; and never two ladies loved as they do.

Oliver. Where will the old duke live? 109

Charles. They say he is already in the forest of Arden, and a many merry men with him; and there they live like the old Robin Hood of England. They say many young gentlemen flock to him every day, and fleet the time carelessly, as they did in the golden world.

Oliver. What, you wrestle to-morrow before the new duke? 116

Charles. Marry, do I, sir; and I came to acquaint you with a matter. I am given, sir, secretly to understand that your younger brother Orlando hath a disposition to come in disguised against me to try a fall. To- 120 morrow, sir, I wrestle for my credit, and he that escapes me without some broken limb shall acquit him well. Your brother is but young and tender; and, for your love, I would be loath to foil him as I must, for my own honour, if he come in: therefore, out of my love to 125 you, I came hither to acquaint you withal, that either you might stay him from his intendment, or brook such disgrace well as he shall run into, in that it is a thing of his own search and altogether against my will.

Oliver. Charles, I thank thee for thy love to me, 130 which thou shalt find I will most kindly requite. I had myself notice of my brother's purpose herein, and have

---

106 **to stay**: in staying, if she had stayed.   113 **fleet the time**: make the time flow.   120 **fall**: bout of wrestling.   123–4 **for your love**: for love of you.   124 **foil**: overthrow.   126 **withal**: with it.   127 **stay ... his intendment**: stop him from carrying out his intention.   **brook**: put up with.

by underhand means laboured to dissuade him from it,
but he is resolute. I'll tell thee, Charles, it is the
stubbornest young fellow of France; full of ambition, 135
an envious emulator of every man's good parts, a
secret and villainous contriver against me his natural
brother: therefore use thy discretion. I had as lief
thou didst break his neck as his finger. And thou wert
best look to't; for if thou dost him any slight disgrace, 140
or if he do not mightily grace himself on thee, he will
practise against thee by poison, entrap thee by some
treacherous device, and never leave thee till he hath
ta'en thy life by some indirect means or other; for,
I assure thee,—and almost with tears I speak it,— 145
there is not one so young and so villainous this day
living. I speak but brotherly of him; but should I
anatomize him to thee as he is, I must blush and weep,
and thou must look pale and wonder.   149

Charles. I am heartily glad I came hither to you. If he
come to-morrow, I'll give him his payment: if ever he go
alone again, I'll never wrestle for prize more; and so God
keep your worship!   [*Exit.*

Oliver. Farewell, good Charles. Now will I stir this
gamester. I hope I shall see an end of him; for my 155
soul, yet I know not why, hates nothing more than he.
Yet he's gentle, never schooled and yet learned, full of
noble device, of all sorts enchantingly beloved, and,

---

133 **underhand:** indirectly conveyed [*N*].   137 **natural:** by
birth.   138 **I had as lief:** it would please me as well.   139–
42 **thou wert best . . . poison:** you had better take care, for, if
you harm him slightly, or if he does not succeed handsomely against
you, he will try by some underhand trick to poison you (**practise =**
plot).   148 **anatomize:** describe in detail.   151-2 **go alone:**
walk unaided.   155 **gamester:** athlete (contemptuously).
158 **device:** cast of mind, ideas.   **of all sorts enchantingly**
beloved: loved by all ranks and kinds of men as if he laid them under
a magic charm.

indeed so much in the heart of the world, and
especially of my own people, who best know him, that **160**
I am altogether misprised. But it shall not be so long;
this wrestler shall clear all: nothing remains but that
I kindle the boy thither, which now I'll go about.

Scene II. A LAWN BEFORE THE DUKE'S PALACE.

Enter ROSALIND and CELIA.

Celia. I pray thee, Rosalind, sweet my coz, be merry.

Rosalind. Dear Celia, I show more mirth than I am mis-
stress of, and would you yet I were merrier? Unless you
could teach me to forget a banished father, you must not
learn me how to remember any extraordinary pleasure. **5**

Celia. Herein I see thou lovest me not with the full
weight that I love thee. If my uncle, thy banished
father, had banished thy uncle, the duke my father, so
thou hadst been still with me, I could have taught
my love to take thy father for mine: so wouldst thou, **10**
if the truth of thy love to me were so righteously
tempered as mine is to thee.

Rosalind. Well, I will forget the condition of my estate,
to rejoice in yours.

Celia. You know my father hath no child but I, nor **15**
none is like to have; and, truly, when he dies, thou
shalt be his heir: for what he hath taken away from
thy father perforce, I will render thee again in affec-

---

161 misprised: despised.   **162 clear all:** remove all my
difficulties.   **1 coz:** cousin [*N*].   **2–3 I show . . . of:** I give
the appearance of more mirth than I really have.   **5 learn:**
teach.   **extraordinary pleasure:** pleasure beyond my (present)
capacity for enjoyment.   **8–10 so thou . . . for mine:** provided
you had remained with me, I could have so trained my love (for you)
that it would have accepted your father in place of my own (**so =**
provided).   **11–12 righteously tempered:** properly blended.   **13
estate:** fortunes.

tion; by mine honour, I will; and when I break that
oath, let me turn monster. Therefore, my sweet Rose,   20
my dear Rose, be merry.

Rosalind. From henceforth I will, coz, and devise sports.
Let me see; what think you of falling in love?

Celia. Marry, I prithee, do, to make sport withal: but
love no man in good earnest; nor no further in sport
neither, than with safety of a pure blush thou mayst in
honour come off again.   27

Rosalind. What shall be our sport then?

Celia. Let us sit and mock the good housewife Fortune
from her wheel, that her gifts may henceforth be bestowed
equally.   31

Rosalind. I would we could do so, for her benefits are
mightily misplaced, and the bountiful blind woman doth
most mistake in her gifts to women.

Celia. 'Tis true; for those that she makes fair she scarce
makes honest, and those that she makes honest she makes
very ill-favouredly.   37

Rosalind. Nay, now thou goest from Fortune's office to
Nature's: Fortune reigns in gifts of the world, not in the
lineaments of Nature.

Enter TOUCHSTONE.

Celia. No? when Nature hath made a fair creature, may
she not by Fortune fall into the fire? Though Nature hath
given us wit to flout at Fortune, hath not Fortune sent in
this fool to cut off the argument?   44

Rosalind. Indeed, there is Fortune too hard for Nature,
when Fortune makes Nature's natural the cutter-off of
Nature's wit.

25–7 **nor no further . . . come off again:** give no man, even in
fun, more love than you may safely and honourably escape from with
a mere blush.   30 **from:** away from, i.e. into deserting her wheel
[*N*].   36 **honest:** chaste.   43 **flout:** mock.   46 **natural:** born fool.

Celia. Peradventure this is not Fortune's work neither, but Nature's; who, perceiving our natural wits too dull to reason of such goddesses, hath sent 50 this natural for our whetstone: for always the dulness of the fool is the whetstone of the wits. How now, wit! whither wander you?

Touchstone. Mistress, you must come away to your father.

Celia. Were you made the messenger? 55

Touchstone. No, by mine honour; but I was bid to come for you.

Rosalind. Where learned you that oath, fool?

Touchstone. Of a certain knight that swore by his honour they were good pancakes, and swore by his honour the mustard was naught: now, I'll stand to it, the pancakes were naught and the mustard was good, and yet was not the knight forsworn. 63

Celia. How prove you that, in the great heap of your knowledge?

Rosalind. Ay, marry: now unmuzzle your wisdom.

Touchstone. Stand you both forth now: stroke your chins, and swear by your beards that I am a knave.

Celia. By our beards,—if we had them,—thou art. 69

Touchstone. By my knavery,—if I had it,—then I were; but if you swear by that that is not, you are not forsworn: no more was this knight, swearing by his honour, for he never had any; or if he had, he had sworn it away before ever he saw those pancakes or that mustard.

Celia. Prithee, who is 't that thou meanest? 75

Touchstone. One that old Frederick, your father, loves.

Celia. My father's love is enough to honour him enough. Speak no more of him; you'll be whipped for taxation one of these days. 79

51–2 **the dulness . . . wits:** a fool's stupidity sharpens a wise man's wits [*N*].   60 **pancakes:** fritters (even of meat, hence the mustard).   78 **taxation:** censure, sarcasm.

Touchstone. The more pity, that fools may not speak wisely what wise men do foolishly.   81

Celia. By my troth, thou sayest true; for since the little wit that fools have was silenced, the little foolery that wise men have makes a great show. Here comes Monsieur Le Beau.   85

Rosalind. With his mouth full of news.

Celia. Which he will put on us, as pigeons feed their young.

Rosalind. Then we shall be news-cramm'd.

Celia. All the better; we shall be more marketable.   90

Enter LE BEAU.

Bon jour, Monsieur Le Beau: what's the news?

Le Beau. Fair princess, you have lost much good sport.

Celia. Sport! Of what colour?

Le Beau. What colour, madam! How shall I answer you?

Rosalind. As wit and fortune will.   95

Touchstone. Or as the Destinies decree.

Celia. Well said: that was laid on with a trowel.

Touchstone. Nay, if I keep not my rank,—

Rosalind. Thou losest thy old smell.

Le Beau. You amaze me, ladies: I would have told you of good wrestling, which you have lost the sight of.   101

Rosalind. Yet tell us the manner of the wrestling.

Le Beau. I will tell you the beginning; and, if it please your ladyships, you may see the end, for the best is yet to do; and here, where you are, they are coming to perform it.   106

Celia. Well, the beginning, that is dead and buried.

Le Beau. There comes an old man and his three sons,—

Celia. I could match this beginning with an old tale.

---

87 put on: force on.   **93 colour:** kind, quality [*N*].   **97**
that was laid on with a trowel: that was cleverly done [*N*].   **100**
amaze: bewilder.

Le Beau. Three proper young men, of excellent growth
and presence;—   111

Rosalind. With bills on their necks, 'Be it known unto
all men by these presents.'

Le Beau. The eldest of the three wrestled with
Charles, the duke's wrestler; which Charles in a 115
moment threw him and broke three of his ribs, that
there is little hope of life in him: so he served the
second, and so the third. Yonder they lie; the poor old
man, their father, making such pitiful dole over them
that all the beholders take his part with weeping.   120

Rosalind. Alas!

Touchstone. But what is the sport, monsieur, that the
ladies have lost?

Le Beau. Why, this that I speak of.   124

Touchstone. Thus men may grow wiser every day: it is
the first time that ever I heard breaking of ribs was sport
for ladies.

Celia. Or I, I promise thee.

Rosalind. But is there any else longs to see this broken
music in his sides? is there yet another dotes upon rib-
breaking? Shall we see this wrestling, cousin?   131

Le Beau. You must, if you stay here; for here is the place
appointed for the wrestling, and they are ready to perform it.

Celia. Yonder, sure, they are coming: let us now stay and
see it.   136

Flourish. Enter DUKE FREDERICK, Lords, ORLANDO,
CHARLES, *and* Attendants.

Duke Frederick. Come on: since the youth will not be
entreated, his own peril on his forwardness.

110 **proper:** handsome.   129–30 **see this broken music in
his sides:** see his sides well bethumped [*N*].   138 **his own peril
on his forwardness:** his danger is the result of his own reckless-
ness.

Rosalind. Is yonder the man?

Le Beau. Even he, madam.   140

Celia. Alas! he is too young: yet he looks successfully.

Duke Frederick. How now, daughter and cousin! are you crept hither to see the wrestling?

Rosalind. Ay, my liege, so please you give us leave. 144

Duke Frederick. You will take little delight in it, I can tell you, there is such odds in the man: in pity of the challenger's youth I would fain dissuade him, but he will not be entreated. Speak to him, ladies; see if you can move him.

Celia. Call him hither, good Monsieur le Beau.   149

Duke Frederick. Do so: I'll not be by. [DUKE *goes apart.*

Le Beau. Monsieur the challenger, the princess calls for you.

Orlando. I attend them with all respect and duty.

Rosalind. Young man, have you challenged Charles the wrestler?   155

Orlando. No, fair princess; he is the general challenger: I come but in, as others do, to try with him the strength of my youth.

Celia. Young gentleman, your spirits are too bold for your years. You have seen cruel proof of this man's 160 strength: if you saw yourself with your eyes or knew yourself with your judgment, the fear of your adventure would counsel you to a more equal enterprise. We pray you, for your own sake, to embrace your own safety and give over this attempt.   165

Rosalind. Do, young sir: your reputation shall not therefore be misprised. We will make it our suit to the duke that the wrestling might not go forward.

Orlando. I beseech you, punish me not with your

141 **successfully:** like a winner.   146 **odds:** superiority (of Charles).   161–3 **if you saw . . . equal enterprise:** if you saw and judged yourself truly, then you would not be so rash as to challenge an adversary so far beyond your capacity.

hard thoughts, wherein I confess me much guilty, to 170
deny so fair and excellent ladies anything. But let
your fair eyes and gentle wishes go with me to my trial:
wherein if I be foiled, there is but one shamed that was
never gracious; if killed, but one dead that is willing to
be so. I shall do my friends no wrong, for I have none 175
to lament me; the world no injury, for in it I have
nothing; only in the world I fill up a place, which may
be better supplied when I have made it empty.

Rosalind. The little strength that I have, I would it
were with you.   180

Celia. And mine, to eke out hers.

Rosalind. Fare you well. Pray heaven I be deceived in you!

Celia. Your heart's desires be with you!

Charles. Come, where is this young gallant that is so
desirous to lie with his mother earth?   185

Orlando. Ready, sir; but his will hath in it a more
modest working.

Duke Frederick. You shall try but one fall.

Charles. No, I warrant your Grace, you shall not entreat
him to a second, that have so mightily persuaded him from
a first.   191

Orlando. You mean to mock me after; you should not
have mocked me before: but come your ways.

Rosalind. Now Hercules be thy speed, young man! 194

Celia. I would I were invisible, to catch the strong
fellow by the leg.   [CHARLES *and* ORLANDO *wrestle.*

Rosalind. O excellent young man!

Celia. If I had a thunderbolt in mine eye, I can tell who
should down.   [CHARLES *is thrown. Shout.*

---

174 **gracious**: favoured, popular.   182 **I be deceived in you:**
i.e. you prove more successful than I expect.   186–7 **more modest
working**: less pretentious attempt, i.e. I am content to throw you
to the ground.   194 **be thy speed**: bring thee good fortune [N].
199 **down**: be thrown.

B

Duke Frederick. No more, no more.   200

Orlando. Yes, I beseech your Grace: I am not yet well
breathed.

Duke Frederick. How dost thou, Charles?

Le Beau. He cannot speak, my lord.   204

Duke Frederick. Bear him away. What is thy name,
young man?   [CHARLES *is borne out.*

Orlando. Orlando, my liege; the youngest son of Sir
Rowland de Boys.   208

Duke Frederick. I would thou hadst been son to some
    man else:

The world esteem'd thy father honourable,   210
But I did find him still mine enemy:
Thou shouldst have better pleas'd me with this deed,
Hadst thou descended from another house.
But fare thee well; thou art a gallant youth:
I would thou hadst told me of another father.   215

              [*Exeunt* DUKE FREDERICK, *Train, and* LE BEAU.

Celia. Were I my father, coz, would I do this?

Orlando. I am more proud to be Sir Rowland's son,
His youngest son; and would not change that calling,
To be adopted heir to Frederick.

Rosalind. My father lov'd Sir Rowland as his soul,   220
And all the world was of my father's mind:
Had I before known this young man his son,
I should have given him tears unto entreaties,
Ere he should thus have ventur'd.

Celia.   Gentle cousin,
Let us go thank him and encourage him: 225
My father's rough and envious disposition
Sticks me at heart. Sir, you have well deserv'd:
If you do keep your promises in love

201–2 **I am ... breathed:** I have not yet found my wind.   211
still: always.   218 **calling:** title [*N*].   227 **sticks:** stabs, or
(perhaps) is a *fixed* pain.

But justly, as you have exceeded all promise,
Your mistress shall be happy.
  Rosalind.   Gentleman,   230
             [*Giving him a chain from her neck.*
Wear this for me, one out of suits with fortune,
That could give more, but that her hand lacks means.
Shall we go, coz?
  Celia.   Ay. Fare you well, fair gentleman.
  Orlando. Can I not say, I thank you? My better parts
Are all thrown down, and that which here stands up   235
Is but a quintain, a mere lifeless block.
  Rosalind. He calls us back: my pride fell with **my**
    fortunes;
I'll ask him what he would. Did you call, sir?
Sir, you have wrestled well, and overthrown
More than your enemies.
  Celia.   Will you go, coz?   240
  Rosalind. Have with you. Fare you well.
              [*Exeunt* ROSALIND *and* CELIA.
  Orlando. What passion hangs these weights upon **my**
    tongue?
I cannot speak to her, yet she urg'd conference.
O poor Orlando, thou art overthrown!
Or Charles or something weaker masters thee.   245

Re-enter LE BEAU.

  Le Beau. Good sir, I do in friendship counsel you
To leave this place. Albeit you have deserv'd
High commendation, true applause and love,
Yet such is now the duke's condition
That he misconsters all that you have done.   250

231 **out of suits with fortune:** no longer favoured by fortune
[*N*].   232 **could give:** would like to give.   236 **quintain:**
a figure at which to tilt [*N*].   241 **Have with you:** I'm coming.
243 **conference:** conversation.   245 **something weaker:**
i.e. a woman.   250 **misconsters:** misconstrues [*N*].

The duke is humorous: what he is indeed,
More suits you to conceive than I to speak of.

Orlando. I thank you, sir; and pray you, tell me this;
Which of the two was daughter of the duke,
That here was at the wrestling?   255

Le Beau. Neither his daughter, if we judge by manners:
But yet, indeed the smaller is his daughter:
The other is daughter to the banish'd duke,
And here detain'd by her usurping uncle,
To keep his daughter company; whose loves   260
Are dearer than the natural bond of sisters.
But I can tell you that of late this duke
Hath ta'en displeasure 'gainst his gentle niece,
Grounded upon no other argument
But that the people praise her for her virtues,   265
And pity her for her good father's sake;
And, on my life, his malice 'gainst the lady
Will suddenly break forth. Sir, fare you well:
Hereafter, in a better world than this,
I shall desire more love and knowledge of you.   270

Orlando. I rest much bounden to you: fare you well.

[*Exit* LE BEAU.

Thus must I from the smoke into the smother;
From tyrant duke unto a tyrant brother.
But heavenly Rosalind!   [*Exit.*

Scene III. A ROOM IN THE PALACE

Enter CELIA *and* ROSALIND.

Celia. Why, cousin! why, Rosalind! Cupid have mercy!
Not a word?

Rosalind. Not one to throw at a dog.

251 **humorous**: obdurate of temper [N].   260 **whose**: their.
264 **argument**: cause.   269 **in a better world than this**: when
things are going better than now.   271 **bounden**: indebted.
272 **smother**: thick smoke; i.e. out of the frying-pan into the fire.

Celia. No, thy words are too precious to be cast away upon curs; throw some of them at me; come, lame me with reasons.   6

Rosalind. Then there were two cousins laid up; when the one should be lamed with reasons and the other mad without any.

Celia. But is all this for your father?   10

Rosalind. No, some of it is for my child's father: O, how full of briers is this working-day world!

Celia. They are but burrs, cousin, thrown upon thee in holiday foolery: if we walk not in the trodden paths, our very petticoats will catch them.   15

Rosalind. I could shake them off my coat: these burrs are in my heart.

Celia. Hem them away.

Rosalind. I would try, if I could cry 'hem', and have him.   20

Celia. Come, come; wrestle with thy affections.

Rosalind. O! they take the part of a better wrestler than myself!   23

Celia. O, a good wish upon you! you will try in time, in despite of a fall. But, turning these jests out of service, let us talk in good earnest: is it possible, on such a sudden, you should fall into so strong a liking with old Sir Rowland's youngest son?

Rosalind. The duke my father loved his father dearly. 29

Celia. Doth it therefore ensue that you should love his son dearly? By this kind of chase, I should hate him, for my father hated his father dearly; yet I hate not Orlando.

Rosalind. No, faith, hate him not, for my sake.

---

13 **burrs**: prickly seed-case of plants.   16 **coat**: petticoat.
18 **hem**: cough.   24 **a good wish upon you**: my blessing on you, or good luck!   25 **turning . . . service**: dismissing (like a servant).   31 **chase**: logical sequence.   32 **dearly**: intensely
[*N*].

Celia. Why should I not? doth he not deserve well?

Rosalind. Let me love him for that; and do you love him,
because I do. Look, here comes the duke.   36

Celia. With his eyes full of anger.

Enter DUKE FREDERICK, *with* Lords.

Duke Frederick. Mistress, dispatch you with your safest
      haste,
And get you from our court.

Rosalind.   Me, uncle?

Duke Frederick.   You, cousin:
Within these ten days if that thou be'st found   40
So near our public court as twenty miles,
Thou diest for it.

Rosalind.   I do beseech your Grace,
Let me the knowledge of my fault bear with me,
If with myself I hold intelligence,
Or have acquaintance with mine own desires,   45
If that I do not dream or be not frantic,—
As I do trust I am not,—then, dear uncle,
Never so much as in a thought unborn
Did I offend your highness.

Duke Frederick.   Thus do all traitors:
If their purgation did consist in words,   50
They are as innocent as grace itself:
Let it suffice thee that I trust thee not.

Rosalind. Yet your mistrust cannot make me a traitor:
Tell me whereon the likelihood depends.

Duke Frederick. Thou art thy father's daughter; there's
      enough.   55

38 safest haste: speed that will ensure complete safety.   **39
cousin:** relation by blood or marriage, here niece.   **44 with
myself . . . intelligence:** understand my own mind.   **50
purgation:** exculpation [N].   **54 likelihood:** probability (that
I am a traitor as you think).

Rosalind. So was I when your highness took his dukedom;
So was I when your highness banish'd him,
Treason is not inherited, my lord;
Or, if we did derive it from our friends,
What's that to me? my father was no traitor: 60
Then, good my liege, mistake me not so much
To think my poverty is treacherous.

  Celia. Dear sovereign, hear me speak.

  Duke Frederick. Ay, Celia; we stay'd her for your
    sake;
Else had she with her father rang'd along.   65

  Celia. I did not then entreat to have her stay;
It was your pleasure and your own remorse,
I was too young that time to value her;
But now I know her: if she be a traitor,
Why so am I; we still have slept together,   70
Rose at an instant, learn'd, play'd, eat together;
And wheresoe'er we went, like Juno's swans,
Still we went coupled and inseparable.

  Duke Frederick. She is too subtle for thee; and her
    smoothness,
Her very silence and her patience,   75
Speak to the people, and they pity her.
Thou art a fool: she robs thee of thy name;
And thou wilt show more bright and seem more virtuous
When she is gone. Then open not thy lips:
Firm and irrevocable is my doom   80
Which I have pass'd upon her; she is banish'd.

  Celia. Pronounce that sentence then on me, my liege:
I cannot live out of her company.

61–2 **mistake ... treacherous:** do not form so wrong an opinion
of me as to think I am a traitor merely because I am poor.   65
rang'd: gone wandering, roved.   67 **remorse:** compassion.
70 **still:** always.   77 **robs thee of thy name:** steals the prestige
due to you.

Duke Frederick. You are a fool. You, niece, provide
　　yourself:
If you outstay the time, upon mine honour,   85
And in the greatness of my word, you die.

　　　　　　　　　　[*Exeunt* DUKE FREDERICK *and* Lords.

　Celia. O my poor Rosalind! whither wilt thou go?
Wilt thou change fathers? I will give thee mine.
I charge thee, be not thou more griev'd than I am.
　Rosalind. I have more cause.
　Celia.　　　　　　　　　Thou hast not, cousin; 90
Prithee, be cheerful; know'st thou not, the duke
Hath banish'd me, his daughter?
　Rosalind.　　　　　　　That he hath not.
　Celia. No, hath not? Rosalind lacks then the love
Which teacheth thee that thou and I am one:
Shall we be sunder'd? shall we part, sweet girl?   95
No: let my father seek another heir.
Therefore devise with me how we may fly,
Whither to go, and what to bear with us:
And do not seek to take your change upon you,
To bear your griefs yourself and leave me out;   100
For, by this heaven, now at our sorrows pale,
Say what thou canst, I'll go along with thee.
　Rosalind. Why, whither shall we go?
　Celia. To seek my uncle in the forest of Arden,
　Rosalind. Alas, what danger will it be to us,   105
Maids as we are, to travel forth so far!
Beauty provoketh thieves sooner than gold.
　Celia. I'll put myself in poor and mean attire,
And with a kind of umber smirch my face;
The like do you: so shall we pass along   110
And never stir assailants.

　84 **provide yourself:** prepare for departure.   86 **in the
greatness:** on the authority.   109 **umber:** brown, or a brown
earth used as a pigment.

Rosalind.   Were it not better,
Because that I am more than common tall,
That I did suit me all points like a man?
A gallant curtle-axe upon my thigh,
A boar-spear in my hand; and,—in my heart   115
Lie there what hidden woman's fear there will,—
We'll have a swashing and a martial outside,
As many other mannish cowards have
That do outface it with their semblances.

Celia. What shall I call thee when thou art a man?   120

Rosalind. I'll have no worse a name than Jove's own
    page,
And therefore look you call me Ganymede.
But what will you be call'd?

Celia. Something that hath a reference to my state:
No longer Celia, but Aliena.   125

Rosalind. But, cousin, what if we assay'd to steal
The clownish fool out of your father's court?
Would he not be a comfort to our travel?

Celia. He'll go along o'er the wide world with me;
Leave me alone to woo him. Let's away,   130
And get our jewels and our wealth together,
Devise the fittest time and safest way
To hide us from pursuit that will be made
After my flight. Now go we in content   134
To liberty and not to banishment.   [*Exeunt.*

113 **suit me:** dress myself.   114 **curtle-axe:** cutlass, short
sword.   117 **swashing:** swaggering (giving the appearance of
bravery).   118 **mannish cowards:** cowardly men.   119
semblances: feigned appearances [*N*].

ACT II

Scene I. THE FOREST OF ARDEN

Enter DUKE *Senior,* AMIENS, *and other* Lords, *like Foresters.*

Duke Senior. Now, my co-mates and brothers in exile,
Hath not old custom made this life more sweet
Than that of painted pomp? Are not these woods
More free from peril than the envious court?
Here feel we not the penalty of Adam?   **5**
The seasons' difference,—as, the icy fang
And churlish chiding of the winter's wind,
Which, when it bites and blows upon my body,
Even till I shrink with cold, I smile and say
'This is no flattery: these are counsellors   **10**
That feelingly persuade me what I am.'
Sweet are the uses of adversity,
Which like the toad, ugly and venomous,
Wears yet a precious jewel in his head;
And this our life exempt from public haunt,   **15**
Finds tongues in trees, books in the running brooks,
Sermons in stones, and good in every thing.
   Amiens. I would not change it. Happy is your Grace,
That can translate the stubbornness of fortune
Into so quiet and so sweet a style.   **20**
   Duke Senior. Come, shall we go and kill us venison?
And yet it irks me the poor dappled fools,
Being native burghers of this desert city,

---

2 old custom: our long acquaintance with it.   **6 as:** for
example.   **11 feelingly persuade me:** make me aware through my
senses, or (perhaps) keenly aware.   **12 uses:** benefits.   **15
exempt from public haunt:** free from crowds.   **22 irks me:**
troubles me that.   **23 desert city:** i.e. the forest.

Should in their own confines with forked heads
Have their round haunches gor'd.

    First Lord.   Indeed, my lord,   **25**
The melancholy Jaques grieves at that;
And, in that kind, swears you do more usurp
Than doth your brother that hath banish'd you.
To-day my Lord of Amiens and myself
Did steal behind him as he lay along   **80**
Under an oak whose antique root peeps out
Upon the brook that brawls along this wood;
To the which place a poor sequester'd stag,
That from the hunters' aim had ta'en a hurt,
Did come to languish; and, indeed, my lord,   **85**
The wretched animal heav'd forth such groans
That their discharge did stretch his leathern coat
Almost to bursting, and the big round tears
Cours'd one another down his innocent nose
In piteous chase; and thus the hairy fool,   **40**
Much marked of the melancholy Jaques,
Stood on the extremest verge of the swift brook,
Augmenting it with tears.

    Duke Senior.   But what said Jaques?
Did he not moralize this spectacle?

    First Lord. O, yes, into a thousand similes.   **45**
First, for his weeping into the needless stream;
'Poor deer,' quoth he, 'thou mak'st a testament
As worldlings do, giving thy sum of more
To that which had too much:' then, being there alone,

---

24 **confines**: territory.   **forked heads**: arrows.   **27 in that kind**: in that respect.   33 **sequester'd**: isolated (from the rest of the herd).   40 **fool**: poor creature [*N*].   **44 moralize**: expound, make it the text for a discourse.   **45 similes**: comparisons.   46 **needless**: active sense, i.e. stream that has no need.   47 **testament**: will.   48–9 **As worldlings . . . much**: like worldly people, you are bequeathing more to those who had too much before.

Left and abandon'd of his velvet friends;   50
''Tis right,' quoth he; 'thus misery doth part
The flux of company:' anon, a careless herd,
Full of the pasture, jumps along by him
And never stays to greet him; 'Ay,' quoth Jaques,
'Sweep on, you fat and greasy citizens;   55
'Tis just the fashion; wherefore do you look
Upon that poor and broken bankrupt there?'
Thus most invectively he pierceth through
The body of the country, city, court,
Yea, and of this our life; swearing that we   60
Are mere usurpers, tyrants, and what's worse,
To fright the animals and to kill them up
In their assign'd and native dwelling-place.
    Duke Senior. And did you leave him in this contemplation?
    Second Lord. We did, my lord, weeping and commenting
Upon the sobbing deer.
    Duke Senior.   Show me the place.   66
I love to cope him in these sullen fits,
For then he's full of matter.
    Second Lord. I'll bring you to him straight.   [*Exeunt.*

Scene II. A ROOM IN THE PALACE

Enter DUKE FREDERICK, Lords, *and* Attendants.

Duke Frederick. Can it be possible that no man saw them?
It cannot be: some villains of my court
Are of consent and sufferance in this.

50 **velvet:** soft-coated.   51–2 **part the flux of company:** leave the crowded throng.   52 **herd:** i.e. of deer.   58–9 **Thus . . . court:** thus he attacks and keenly analyses the state of the country, the city, and the court.   61 **mere:** nothing less than, absolute. 67 **cope:** encounter.   68 **matter:** good sense, things worth hearing.   3 **Are of consent and sufferance:** have connived.

First Lord. I cannot hear of any that did see her.
The ladies, her attendants of her chamber,   5
Saw her a-bed; and, in the morning early
They found the bed untreasur'd of their mistress.
  Second Lord. My lord, the roynish clown, at whom so oft
Your Grace was wont to laugh, is also missing.
Hisperia, the princess' gentlewoman,   10
Confesses that she secretly o'erheard
Your daughter and her cousin much commend
The parts and graces of the wrestler
That did but lately foil the sinewy Charles;
And she believes, wherever they are gone,   15
That youth is surely in their company.
  Duke Frederick. Send to his brother; fetch that gallant hither;
If he be absent, bring his brother to me;
I'll make him find him. Do this suddenly,
And let not search and inquisition quail   20
To bring again these foolish runaways.   [*Exeunt.*

Scene III. BEFORE OLIVER'S HOUSE

Enter ORLANDO *and* ADAM, *meeting.*

Orlando. Who's there?
  Adam. What! my young master? O my gentle master!
O my sweet master! O you memory
Of old Sir Rowland! why, what make you here?
Why are you virtuous? Why do people love you?   5
And wherefore are you gentle, strong, and valiant?
Why would you be so fond to overcome
The bonny priser of the humorous duke?

---

  7 untreasur'd: stripped of its treasure.   **8 roynish:** scurvy,
hence coarse.   **17 that gallant:** that ladies' man, i.e. Orlando.
20 let not . . . inquisition quail: let not inquiry slacken.   **3
memory:** memorial.   **7-8 so fond . . . priser:** so foolish as to
defeat the strong prize-fighter [*N*].

Your praise is come too swiftly home before you.
Know you not, master, to some kind of men   10
Their graces serve them but as enemies?
No more do yours: your virtues, gentle master,
Are sanctified and holy traitors to you.
O, what a world is this, when what is comely
Envenoms him that bears it!   15
  Orlando. Why, what's the matter?
  Adam.   O unhappy youth!
Come not within these doors; within this roof
The enemy of all your graces lives.
Your brother,—no, no brother; yet the son,—
Yet not the son, I will not call him son   20
Of him I was about to call his father,—
Hath heard your praises, and this night he means
To burn the lodging where you use to lie,
And you within it: if he fail of that,
He will have other means to cut you off.   25
I overheard him and his practices.
This is no place; this house is but a butchery:
Abhor it, fear it, do not enter it.
  Orlando. Why, whither, Adam, wouldst thou have me go?
  Adam. No matter whither, so you come not here.   30
  Orlando. What! wouldst thou have me go and beg my
    food?
Or with a base and boisterous sword enforce
A thievish living on the common road?
This I must do, or know not what to do:
Yet this I will not do, do how I can;   35
I rather will subject me to the malice

---

12 **No more do yours:** your good gifts do you no more good
than theirs, i.e. your bravery has only got you into trouble. 17
roof: house.   23 **use to lie:** are accustomed to sleep.   26
practices: plots.   27 **butchery:** shambles.   32-3 **with a base
... common road:** i.e. turn highwayman.

Of a diverted blood and bloody brother.

   Adam. But do not so. I have five hundred crowns,
The thrifty hire I sav'd under your father,
Which I did store to be my foster-nurse   40
When service should in my old limbs lie lame,
And unregarded age in corners thrown.
Take that; and He that doth the ravens feed,
Yea, providently caters for the sparrow,
Be comfort to my age! Here is the gold;   45
All this I give you. Let me be your servant:
Though I look old, yet I am strong and lusty;
For in my youth I never did apply
Hot and rebellious liquors in my blood,
Nor did not with unbashful forehead woo   50
The means of weakness and debility;
Therefore my age is as a lusty winter,
Frosty, but kindly. Let me go with you;
I'll do the service of a younger man
In all your business and necessities.   55

   Orlando. O good old man! how well in thee appears
The constant service of the antique world,
When service sweat for duty, not for meed!
Thou art not for the fashion of these times,
Where none will sweat but for promotion,   60
And having that, do choke their service up
Even with the having: it is not so with thee.
But, poor old man, thou prun'st a rotten tree,

---

   37 **diverted blood**: a blood-relationship turned out of its natural
course (of affection).   39 **thrifty hire**: careful savings out of my
wages.   40 **to be my foster-nurse**: to support, to feed and cherish
me [*N*].   42 **unregarded age in corners thrown**: an old servant
be treated like a worn-out utensil thrown into a corner.   50-1 **Nor
did not . . . debility**: did not indulge in wild pleasures that bring
ill health and loss of strength [*N*].   58 **sweat**: sweated.   61-2
having that . . . having: i.e. when they are promoted, their promotion puts an end to the service which gained it.

That cannot so much as a blossom yield,
In lieu of all thy pains and husbandry.   65
But come thy ways, we'll go along together,
And ere we have thy youthful wages spent,
We'll light upon some settled low content.

  Adam. Master, go on, and I will follow thee
To the last gasp with truth and loyalty.   70
From seventeen years till now almost fourscore
Here lived I, but now live here no more.
At seventeen years many their fortunes seek;
But at fourscore it is too late a week:
Yet fortune cannot recompense me better   75
Than to die well and not my master's debtor.   [*Exeunt.*

Scene *IV*. The Forest of Arden

Enter ROSALIND *in boy's clothes,* CELIA *dressed like a*
shepherdess, and TOUCHSTONE.

  Rosalind. O Jupiter! how weary are my spirits.

  Touchstone. I care not for my spirits if my legs were not
weary.   3

  Rosalind. I could find in my heart to disgrace my man's
apparel and to cry like a woman; but I must comfort the
weaker vessel, as doublet and hose ought to show itself
courageous to petticoat: therefore, courage, good Aliena.

  Celia. I pray you, bear with me: I cannot go no further.

  Touchstone. For my part, I had rather bear with you
than bear you; yet I should bear no cross if I did bear you,
for I think you have no money in your purse.   11

  Rosalind. Well, this is the forest of Arden.

  Touchstone. Ay, now am I in Arden; the more fool I:
when I was at home, I was in a better place: but travellers
must be content.   15

---

  65 In lieu of: in return for.   **68 settled low content**: fixed,
though humble way of life to content us.

Rosalind. Ay, be so, good Touchstone. Look you, who comes here; a young man and an old in solemn talk.

Enter CORIN *and* SILVIUS.

Corin. That is the way to make her scorn you still.
Silvius. O Corin, that thou knew'st how I do love her!
Corin. I partly guess, for I have lov'd ere now.   20
Silvius. No, Corin; being old, thou canst not guess,
Though in thy youth thou wast as true a lover
As ever sigh'd upon a midnight pillow:
But if thy love were ever like to mine,—
As sure I think did never man love so,—   25
How many actions most ridiculous
Hast thou been drawn to by thy fantasy?
Corin. Into a thousand that I have forgotten.
Silvius. O! thou didst then ne'er love so heartily.
If thou remember'st not the slightest folly   30
That ever love did make thee run into,
Thou hast not lov'd:
Or if thou hast not sat as I do now,
Wearing thy hearer in thy mistress' praise,
Thou hast not lov'd: 35
Or if thou hast not broke from company
Abruptly, as my passion now makes me,
Thou hast not lov'd. O Phebe, Phebe, Phebe! [*Exit.*
Rosalind. Alas, poor shepherd! searching of thy wound,
I have by hard adventure found mine own.   40
Touchstone. And I mine. I remember, when I was in love I broke my sword upon a stone, and bid him take that for coming a-night to Jane Smile; and I remember the kissing of her batler, and the cow's dugs that her

27 **fantasy:** love, affection.   34 **Wearing:** tiring [*N*].   39
searching of: probing.   40 **adventure:** chance [*N*].   42 **him:**
i.e. the supposed rival in Jane Smile's affections.   43 **a-night:**
by night [*N*].   44 **batler:** a washing 'dolly', a wooden club for
beating clothes in washing.

pretty chopped hands had milked; and I remember the   45
wooing of a peascod instead of her, from whom I took
two cods, and giving her them again, said with weeping
tears, 'Wear these for my sake.' We that are true
lovers run into strange capers; but as all is mortal in
nature, so is all nature in love mortal in folly.   50

Rosalind. Thou speakest wiser than thou art ware of.

Touchstone. Nay, I shall ne'er be ware of mine own wit
till I break my shins against it.

Rosalind. Jove, Jove! this shepherd's passion
         Is much upon my fashion.   55

Touchstone. And mine; but it grows something stale
with me.

Celia. I pray you, one of you question yond man,
If he for gold will give us any food:
I faint almost to death.

Touchstone.   Holla, you clown!   60

Rosalind. Peace, fool: he's not thy kinsman.

Corin.   Who calls?

Touchstone. Your betters, sir.

Corin.   Else are they very wretched.

Rosalind. Peace, I say. Good even to you, friend.

Corin. And to you, gentle sir, and to you all.

Rosalind. I prithee, shepherd, if that love or gold   65
Can in this desert place buy entertainment,
Bring us where we may rest ourselves and feed.
Here's a young maid with travel much oppress'd,
And faints for succour.

Corin.   Fair sir, I pity her,
And wish, for her sake more than for mine own,   70
My fortunes were more able to relieve her;
But I am shepherd to another man,

---

45 **chopped:** chapped.   46 **peascod:** pod of peas.   50
mortal in folly: extremely foolish [N].   51 **ware:** aware.   52
ware: cautious.

And do not shear the fleeces that I graze:
My master is of churlish disposition
And little recks to find the way to heaven   75
By doing deeds of hospitality.
Besides, his cote, his flocks, and bounds of feed
Are now on sale; and at our sheepcote now,
By reason of his absence, there is nothing
That you will feed on; but what is, come see,   80
And in my voice most welcome shall you be.

Rosalind. What is he that shall buy his flock and pasture?

Corin. That young swain that you saw here but erewhile,
That little cares for buying anything.

Rosalind. I pray thee, if it stand with honesty,   85
Buy thou the cottage, pasture, and the flock,
And thou shalt have to pay for it of us.

Celia. And we will mend thy wages. I like this place,
And willingly could waste my time in it.

Corin. Assuredly the thing is to be sold: 90
Go with me: if you like upon report
The soil, the profit, and this kind of life,
I will your very faithful feeder be,
And buy it with your gold right suddenly.   [*Exeunt.*

Scene V. ANOTHER PART OF THE FOREST

Enter AMIENS, JAQUES, *and Others,*

SONG

Amiens.   Under the greenwood tree
Who loves to lie with me,
And turn his merry note
Unto the sweet bird's throat;

75 recks: cares.   **77 cote:** a shepherd's little cabin.   **bounds of feed:** extent of pasture.   **81 in my voice:** as far as I have a say in it.   **83 erewhile:** a short time ago.   **84 little cares for buying anything:** i.e. is too love-lorn to care.   **85 stand with honesty:** agree with honour, be honourable.   **93 feeder:** shepherd.   **3 turn:** adapt, shape.

> Come hither, come hither, come hither: **5**
> Here shall he see
> No enemy
> But winter and rough weather.

Jaques. More, more, I prithee, more.   **9**

Amiens. It will make you melancholy, Monsieur Jaques.

Jaques. I thank it. More! I prithee, more. I can suck melancholy out of a song as a weasel sucks eggs. More! I prithee, more.   **13**

Amiens. My voice is ragged; I know I cannot please you.

Jaques. I do not desire you to please me; I do desire you to sing. Come, more; another stanzo: call you 'em stanzos?

Amiens. What you will, Monsieur Jaques.

Jaques. Nay, I care not for their names; they owe me nothing. Will you sing?   **20**

Amiens. More at your request than to please myself.

Jaques. Well then, if ever I thank any man, I'll thank you: but that they call compliment is like the encounter of two dog-apes, and when a man thanks me heartily, methinks I have given him a penny and he renders me the beggarly thanks. Come, sing; and you that will not, hold your tongues.   **27**

Amiens. Well, I'll end the song. Sirs, cover the while; the duke will drink under this tree. He hath been all this day to look you.   **30**

Jaques. And I have been all this day to avoid him. He is too disputable for my company: I think of as many matters as he, but I give heaven thanks, and make no boast of them. Come, warble; come.

---

14 ragged: broken, rough.   **16 stanzo:** stanza [N].   **24 dog-apes:** dog-faced baboons.   **26 beggarly:** profuse, like a beggar's.   **28 cover:** lay covers (Fr. *couvert*), lay a table fully for a meal.   **30 look:** look for.   **32 disputable:** disputatious.

SONG

Amiens.   Who doth ambition shun,   [*All together here.*
              And loves to live i' the sun,   36
              Seeking the food he eats,
              And pleas'd with what he gets,
          Come hither, come hither, come hither:
                  Here shall he see   40
                  No enemy
              But winter and rough weather.

Jaques. I'll give you a verse to this note, that I made yesterday in despite of my invention.
Amiens. And I'll sing it.   45
Jaques. Thus it goes:

                  If it do come to pass
                  That any man turn ass,
                  Leaving his wealth and ease,
                  A stubborn will to please,   50
              Ducdame, ducdame, ducdame:
                  Here shall he see
                  Gross fools as he,
              An if he will come to me.

Amiens. What's that 'ducdame'?   55
Jaques. 'Tis a Greek invocation to call fools into a circle. I'll go sleep if I can; if I cannot, I'll rail against all the first-born of Egypt.   58
Amiens. And I'll go seek the duke: his banquet is prepared.   [*Exeunt severally.*

---

37 **seeking . . . eats:** getting his own food, by hunting, &c.
43 **note:** tune.   44 **in despite of my invention:** in spite of my imagination (which refused to work).   51 **Ducdame:** a call or invocation [*N*]   54 **an if:** if (an = if).   59 **banquet:** light meal of fruit and wine, often served as dessert after dinner.

Scene VI. ANOTHER PART OF THE FOREST

Enter ORLANDO *and* ADAM.

Adam. Dear master, I can go no further: O! I die for food. Here lie I down, and measure out my grave. Farewell, kind master.

Orlando. Why, how now, Adam! no greater heart in thee? Live a little; comfort a little; cheer thyself a   5 little. If this uncouth forest yield anything savage, I will either be food for it, or bring it for food to thee. Thy conceit is nearer death than thy powers. For my sake be comfortable, hold death awhile at the arm's end, I will here be with thee presently, and if I bring   10 thee not something to eat, I will give thee leave to die; but if thou diest before I come, thou art a mocker of my labour. Well said! thou lookest cheerly, and I'll be with thee quickly. Yet thou liest in the bleak air: come I will bear thee to some shelter, and thou shalt not die   15 for lack of a dinner, if there live anything in this desert. Cheerly, good Adam.   [*Exeunt.*

Scene VII. ANOTHER PART OF THE FOREST

A table set out. Enter DUKE *Senior,* AMIENS, Lords *like Outlaws.*

Duke Senior. I think he be transform'd into a beast, For I can nowhere find him like a man.

First Lord. My lord, he is but even now gone hence: Here was he merry, hearing of a song.

---

  5 **comfort:** take comfort.   6 **uncouth:** rough, wild.   8 **Thy conceit . . . powers:** you imagine yourself more nearly dead than you really are (**conceit** = thought).   9 **comfortable:** cheerful, of good comfort.   10 **presently:** immediately.   13 **Well said!:** Well done!   **cheerly:** cheerfully (cf. 'good cheer').   3 **but even now:** this very moment.

Duke Senior. If he, compact of jars, grow musical,   5
We shall have shortly discord in the spheres.
Go, seek him: tell him I would speak with him.
　　First Lord. He saves my labour by his own approach.

　　　　　　Enter JAQUES.

Duke Senior. Why, how now, monsieur! what a life
　　is this,
That your poor friends must woo your company?   10
What, you look merrily!
　　Jaques. A fool, a fool! I met a fool i' the forest,
A motley fool; a miserable world!
As I do live by food, I met a fool;
Who laid him down and bask'd him in the sun,   15
And rail'd on Lady Fortune in good terms,
In good set terms, and yet a motley fool.
'Good morrow, fool,' quoth I. 'No, sir,' quoth he,
'Call me not fool till heaven hath sent me fortune.'
And then he drew a dial from his poke,   20
And, looking on it with lack-lustre eye,
Says very wisely, 'It is ten o'clock;
Thus we may see,' quoth he, 'how the world wags;
'Tis but an hour ago since it was nine,
And after one hour more 'twill be eleven;   25
And so, from hour to hour we ripe and ripe,
And then from hour to hour we rot and rot,
And thereby hangs a tale.' When I did hear
The motley fool thus moral on the time,
My lungs began to crow like chanticleer,   30

---

5 compact of jars: composed of discords.　　**6 We shall . . .
spheres:** i.e. everything will be reversed [*N*].　　**13 a motley fool:**
a fool in his professional costume, garments of different colours.
16 good terms: eloquent words (of blame).　　**20 dial:** a portable
sundial (or perhaps a watch).　　**poke:** pouch.　　**29 moral:**
philosophical [*N*].　　**30 crow like chanticleer:** laugh loud and
clear, like a cock's crowing.

That fools should be so deep-contemplative,
And I did laugh sans intermission
An hour by his dial. O noble fool!
A worthy fool! Motley's the only wear.

  Duke Senior. What fool is this?   35

  Jaques. O worthy fool! One that hath been a courtier,
And says, if ladies be but young and fair,
They have the gift to know it; and in his brain,—
Which is as dry as the remainder biscuit
After a voyage,—he hath strange places cramm'd   40
With observation, the which he vents
In mangled forms. O that I were a fool!
I am ambitious for a motley coat.

  Duke Senior. Thou shalt have one.

  Jaques.   It is my only suit;
Provided that you weed your better judgments   45
Of all opinion that grows rank in them
That I am wise. I must have liberty
Withal, as large a charter as the wind,
To blow on whom I please; for so fools have:
And they that are most galled with my folly,   50
They most must laugh. And why, sir, must they so?
The 'why' is plain as way to parish church:
He that a fool doth very wisely hit
Doth very foolishly, although he smart,
Not to seem senseless of the bob; if not,   55
The wise man's folly is anatomiz'd
Even by the squandering glances of the fool.
Invest me in my motley; give me leave
To speak my mind, and I will through and through

---

32 **sans intermission**: without stopping.   39 **remainder**: left over.   40 **places**: topics, or extracts, short passages from books.   41 **vents**: delivers.   44 **suit**: a play upon the two meanings: (i) dress, (ii) petition.   47 **wise**: i.e. to be treated seriously.   48 **large a charter**: generous a permit.   50 **galled**: chafed till the skin breaks.   55 **bob**: taunt, jest [*N*].

Cleanse the foul body of th' infected world,   60
If they will patiently receive my medicine.
   Duke S. Fie on thee! I can tell what thou wouldst do.
   Jaques. What, for a counter, would I do, but good?
   Duke Senior. Most mischievous foul sin, in chiding sin:
For thou thyself hast been a libertine,   65
As sensual as the brutish sting itself;
And all the embossed sores and headed evils,
That thou with licence of free foot hast caught,
Wouldst thou disgorge into the general world.
   Jaques. Why, who cries out on pride,   70
That can therein tax any private party?
Doth it not flow as hugely as the sea,
Till that the weary very means do ebb?
What woman in the city do I name,
When that I say the city-woman bears   75
The cost of princes on unworthy shoulders?
Who can come in and say that I mean her,
When such a one as she such is her neighbour?
Or what is he of basest function,
That says his bravery is not on my cost,—   80
Thinking that I mean him,—but therein suits
His folly to the mettle of my speech?
There then; how then? what then? Let me see wherein
My tongue hath wrong'd him: if it do him right,

63 **What . . . good**: i.e. what harm do you wager I would do? [*N*].
65 **libertine**: free and evil liver.   66 **brutish sting**: impulse of
animal passion.   67 **embossed sores and headed evils**:
swollen, tumid carbuncles and sores grown to a head like a boil.
68 **license . . . foot**: free living.   71 **tax any private party**:
be thought to be censuring any individual [*N*].   78 **such . . .
neighbour**: i.e. her neighbour is such a one as she, just like her.
79–81 **what is he . . . mean him**: i.e. what low menial is there who
thinks I mean him and retorts that I have not to pay for his gaudy
clothes?   81–2 **suits . . . speech**: i.e. shows himself to be the
sort of fool that I have described.   84 **if it do him right**: if my
attack on pride rightly describes him, if the cap fits.

Then he hath wrong'd himself; if he be free,   85
Why then, my taxing like a wild goose flies,
Unclaim'd of any man. But who comes here?

Enter ORLANDO, *with his sword drawn.*

Orlando. Forbear, and eat no more.
Jaques.   Why, I have eat none yet.
Orlando. Nor shalt not, till necessity be serv'd.
Jaques. Of what kind should this cock come of?   90
Duke S. Art thou thus bolden'd, man, by thy distress,
Or else a rude despiser of good manners,
That in civility thou seem'st so empty?
Orlando. You touch'd my vein at first: the thorny point
Of bare distress hath ta'en from me the show   95
Of smooth civility; yet I am inland bred
And know some nurture. But forbear, I say.
He dies that touches any of this fruit
Till I and my affairs are answered.
Jaques. An you will not be answered with reason,   100
I must die.
Duke Senior. What would you have? Your gentleness
    shall force
More than your force move us to gentleness.
Orlando. I almost die for food; and let me have it.
Duke S. Sit down and feed, and welcome to our table. 105
Orlando. Speak you so gently? Pardon me, I pray you:
I thought that all things had been savage here,
And therefore put I on the countenance
Of stern commandment. But whate'er you are
That in this desert inaccessible,   110

---

85 **free**: innocent.   93 **civility**: more than politeness; rather
the courtesy of well-bred people.   94 **You touch'd my vein**: you
described my disposition.   96 **inland bred**: brought up in or
near centres of civilization (as opposed to outlandish).   97
nurture: education, breeding.   99 **answered**: satisfied.

Under the shade of melancholy boughs,
Lose and neglect the creeping hours of time;
If ever you have look'd on better days,
If ever been where bells have knoll'd to church,
If ever sat at any good man's feast,   115
If ever from your eyelids wip'd a tear,
And know what 'tis to pity, and be pitied,
Let gentleness my strong enforcement be:
In the which hope I blush, and hide my sword.

Duke S. True is it that we have seen better days,   120
And have with holy bell been knoll'd to church,
And sat at good men's feasts, and wip'd our eyes
Of drops that sacred pity hath engender'd;
And therefore sit you down in gentleness
And take upon command what help we have   125
That to your wanting may be minister'd.

Orlando. Then but forbear your food a little while,
Whiles, like a doe, I go to find my fawn
And give it food. There is an old poor man,
Who after me hath many a weary step   130
Limp'd in pure love: till he be first suffic'd,
Oppress'd with two weak evils, age and hunger,
I will not touch a bit.

Duke Senior.   Go find him out,
And we will nothing waste till you return.   134

Orlando. I thank ye; and be bless'd for your good com-
          fort!   [*Exit.*

Duke Senior. Thou seest we are not all alone unhappy:
This wide and universal theatre
Presents more woful pageants than the scene
Wherein we play in.

---

114 **knoll'd:** chimed, knelled.   118 **Let gentleness . . . be:**
i.e. let your gentle breeding give force to my request (or my gentleness, &c., cf. l. 124).   125 **upon command:** at your orders.   132
weak evils: evils causing weakness.   134 **waste:** consume.

Jaques.   All the world's a stage,
And all the men and women merely players: **140**
They have their exits and their entrances;
And one man in his time plays many parts,
His acts being seven ages. At first the infant,
Mewling and puking in the nurse's arms.
And then the whining school-boy, with his satchel,   **145**
And shining morning face, creeping like snail
Unwillingly to school. And then the lover,
Sighing like furnace, with a woful ballad
Made to his mistress' eyebrow. Then a soldier,
Full of strange oaths, and bearded like the pard,   **150**
Jealous in honour, sudden and quick in quarrel,
Seeking the bubble reputation
Even in the cannon's mouth. And then the justice,
In fair round belly with good capon lin'd,
With eyes severe, and beard of formal cut,   **155**
Full of wise saws and modern instances;
And so he plays his part. The sixth age shifts
Into the lean and slipper'd pantaloon,
With spectacles on nose and pouch on side,
His youthful hose well sav'd, a world too wide   **160**
For his shrunk shank; and his big manly voice,
Turning again toward childish treble, pipes
And whistles in his sound. Last scene of all,
That ends this strange eventful history,
Is second childishness and mere oblivion,   **165**
Sans teeth, sans eyes, sans taste, sans everything.

---

144 **mewling and puking**: crying and retching [N].   **150**
pard: leopard.   152 **the bubble reputation**: fame empty and
short-lived as a bubble.   154 **In**: appearing with.   **capon**:
young cock [N].   156 **wise saws and modern instances**: wise
sayings (almost proverbs) and trite illustrations.   158 **pantaloon**:
old man approaching senility [N].   163 **his**: its.   165 **mere
oblivion**: utter, complete forgetfulness.

Re-enter ORLANDO, *with* ADAM.

Duke S. Welcome. Set down your venerable burden,
And let him feed.
   Orlando.   I thank you most for him.
   Adam. So had you need:
I scarce can speak to thank you for myself.   170
   Duke Senior. Welcome; fall to: I will not trouble you
As yet, to question you about your fortunes.
Give us some music; and, good cousin, sing.

SONG

Amiens.   Blow, blow, thou winter wind,
        Thou art not so unkind   175
           As man's ingratitude;
        Thy tooth is not so keen,
        Because thou art not seen,
           Although thy breath be rude.
Heigh-ho! sing, heigh-ho! unto the green holly: 180
Most friendship is feigning, most loving mere folly.
        Then heigh-ho! the holly!
        This life is most jolly

        Freeze, freeze, thou bitter sky,
        That dost not bite so nigh   185
           As benefits forgot:
        Though thou the waters warp,
        Thy sting is not so sharp
           As friend remember'd not.
Heigh-ho! sing, heigh-ho! unto the green holly: 190
Most friendship is feigning, most loving mere folly.
        Then heigh-ho! the holly!
        This life is most jolly.

Duke S. If that you were the good Sir Rowland's son,
As you have whisper'd faithfully you were,   195

---

187 **warp:** contract, wrinkle.

And as mine eye doth his effigies witness
Most truly limn'd and living in your face,
Be truly welcome hither: I am the duke
That lov'd your father: the residue of your fortune,
Go to my cave and tell me. Good old man,   **200**
Thou art right welcome as thy master is.
Support him by the arm. Give me your hand,
And let me all your fortunes understand.   [*Exeunt.*

196 **effigies**: likeness.   197 **limn'd**: painted in colours.

ACT III

Scene I. A ROOM IN THE PALACE

Enter DUKE FREDERICK, OLIVER, Lords, *and* Attendants

Duke F. Not see him since! Sir, sir, that cannot be:
But were I not the better part made mercy,
I should not seek an absent argument
Of my revenge, thou present. But look to it:
Find out thy brother, wheresoe'er he is;   5
Seek him with candle; bring him, dead or living,
Within this twelvemonth, or turn thou no more
To seek a living in our territory.
Thy lands and all things that thou dost call thine
Worth seizure, do we seize into our hands,   10
Till thou canst quit thee by thy brother's mouth
Of what we think against thee.
    Oliver. O that your highness knew my heart in this!
I never lov'd my brother in my life.
    Duke F. More villain thou. Well, push him out of doors;
And let my officers of such a nature   16
Make an extent upon his house and lands.
Do this expediently and turn him going.   [*Exeunt.*

Scene II. THE FOREST OF ARDEN

Enter ORLANDO, *with a paper.*

Orlando. Hang there, my verse, in witness of my love:
And thou, thrice-crowned queen of night, survey

2–4 **But were I not . . . thou present:** i.e. if I were not, for the
most part, a merciful man, I would not seek to work out my revenge
on your absent brother while you are here to undergo it (**argument**=
subject).   6 **with candle:** thoroughly [*N*].   7 **turn:** return.
11 **quit:** acquit.   16 **of such a nature:** appointed for that
purpose.   17 **Make an extent:** make a valuation [*N*].   18
expediently: expeditiously.   2 **thrice-crowned queen of night:**
the moon [*N*].

With thy chaste eye, from thy pale sphere above,
   Thy huntress' name, that my full life doth sway.
O Rosalind! these trees shall be my books,   **5**
   And in their barks my thoughts I'll character,
That every eye, which in this forest looks,
   Shall see thy virtue witness'd everywhere.
Run, run, Orlando: carve on every tree
The fair, the chaste, and unexpressive she.   **10**

                      [*Exit.*

Enter CORIN *and* TOUCHSTONE.

Corin. And how like you this shepherd's life, Master
Touchstone?

Touchstone. Truly, shepherd, in respect of itself, it is
a good life; but in respect that it is a shepherd's life, it
is naught. In respect that it is solitary, I like it very **15**
well; but in respect that it is private, it is a very vile
life. Now, in respect it is in the fields, it pleaseth me
well; but in respect it is not in the court, it is tedious.
As it is a spare life, look you, it fits my humour well;
but as there is no more plenty in it, it goes much **20**
against my stomach. Hast any philosophy in thee,
shepherd?

Corin. No more but that I know the more one sickens
the worse at ease he is; and that he that wants money,
means, and content, is without three good friends; that **25**
the property of rain is to wet, and fire to burn; that
good pasture makes fat sheep, and that a great cause
of the night is lack of the sun; that he that hath learned
no wit by nature nor art may complain of good breeding, or comes of a very dull kindred.   **30**

---

   4 full: whole.   **6 character:** write.   **10 unexpressive:**
inexpressible, indescribable.   **15 naught:** worthless.   **19**
humour: disposition.   **25 means:** resources (not necessarily
pecuniary).   **29 complain of:** complain of the lack of.

Touchstone. Such a one is a natural philosopher. Wast ever in court, shepherd?

Corin. No, truly.

Touchstone. Then thou art damned.

Corin. Nay, I hope.   **35**

Touchstone. Truly, thou art damned, like an ill-roasted egg, all on one side.

Corin. For not being at court? Your reason.   **38**

Touchstone. Why, if thou never wast at court, thou never sawest good manners; if thou never sawest good manners, then thy manners must be wicked; and wickedness is sin, and sin is damnation. Thou art in a parlous state, shepherd.

Corin. Not a whit, Touchstone: those that are good manners at the court, are as ridiculous in the country **45** as the behaviour of the country is most mockable at the court. You told me you salute not at the court, but you kiss your hands: that courtesy would be uncleanly if courtiers were shepherds.

Touchstone. Instance, briefly; come, instance.   **50**

Corin. Why, we are still handling our ewes, and their fells, you know, are greasy.

Touchstone. Why, do not your courtier's hands sweat? and is not the grease of a mutton as wholesome as the sweat of a man? Shallow, shallow. A better instance, I say; come.

Corin. Besides, our hands are hard.   **56**

Touchstone. Your lips will feel them the sooner: shallow again. A more sounder instance; come.

31 **natural philosopher:** one who reasons from his observation of nature (with a play on 'natural' meaning 'fool').   **40 manners:** polite behaviour; but in 41 with the older sense of moral character (cf. Lat. *mores*).   42 **parlous:** perilous.   47–8 **but you kiss:** without kissing.   50 **instance:** give your proof.   51 **still:** constantly.   52 **fells:** skins with their wool, also the shorn fleece. 53 **your:** any courtier's, i.e. any of the courtiers I am telling you about.   54 **mutton:** sheep.

Corin. And they are often tarred over with the surgery of our sheep; and would you have us kiss tar? The courtier's hands are perfumed with civet. 61

Touchstone. Most shallow man! Thou worms-meat, in respect of a good piece of flesh, indeed! Learn of the wise, and perpend: civet is of a baser birth than tar, the very uncleanly flux of a cat. Mend the instance, shepherd. 66

Corin. You have too courtly a wit for me: I'll rest.

Touchstone. Wilt thou rest damned? God help thee, shallow man! God make incision in thee! thou art raw. 70

Corin. Sir, I am a true labourer: I earn that I eat, get that I wear, owe no man hate, envy no man's happiness, glad of other men's good, content with my harm; and the greatest of my pride is to see my ewes graze and my lambs suck. 75

Touchstone. That is another simple sin in you, to bring the ewes and the rams together, and to offer to get your living by the copulation of cattle; to be bawd to a bell-wether, and to betray a she-lamb of a twelvemonth to a crooked-pated, old, cuckoldy ram, out of all reason- 80 able match. If thou be'st not damned for this, the devil himself will have no shepherds: I cannot see else how thou shouldst 'scape.

Corin. Here comes young Master Ganymede, my new mistress's brother. 85

---

61 civet: perfume from a gland in a certain species of cat. **62–3 In respect of:** in comparison with. **64 perpend:** consider [*N*]. **69–70 make incision in thee! thou art raw:** improve thee by grafting, for thou art uncultivated [*N*]. **72 owe:** feel towards. **73 content with my harm:** resigned to my sufferings. **76 simple:** plain, mere, or (perhaps) sin due to ignorance. **78 copulation:** pairing. **bawd:** one who makes it a trade to procure a female to satisfy lust (now only applied to a woman). **80–1 out . . . match:** unsuitably.

Enter ROSALIND, *reading a paper.*

Rosalind. From the east to western Ind,
    No jewel is like Rosalind.
Her worth, being mounted on the wind,
    Through all the world bears Rosalind.
All the pictures fairest lin'd   90
    Are but black to Rosalind.
Let no face be kept in mind,
    But the fair of Rosalind.

Touchstone. I'll rime you so, eight years together, dinners and suppers and sleeping hours excepted; it is the right butter-women's rank to market.   96

Rosalind. Out, fool!

Touchstone. For a taste:—

If a hart do lack a hind,
    Let him seek out Rosalind.   100
If the cat will after kind,
    So be sure will Rosalind.
Winter-garments must be lin'd,
    So must slender Rosalind.
They that reap must sheaf and bind,   105
    Then to cart with Rosalind.
Sweetest nut hath sourest rind,
    Such a nut is Rosalind.
He that sweetest rose will find
    Must find love's prick and Rosalind.   110

This is the very false gallop of verses: why do you infect yourself with them?

Rosalind. Peace! you dull fool: I found them on a tree.

Touchstone. Truly, the tree yields bad fruit.   114

Rosalind. I'll graff it with you, and then I shall graff it

90 **lin'd**: sketched, delineated.   93 **fair**: i.e. fair face   95–6 **the right . . . market**: the very jog-trot of butter-women going to market [*N*].   98 **For a taste**: as a specimen.   101 **will after kind**: will run after other cats (a proverbial expression).   115 **graff**: graft.

with a medlar: then it will be the earliest fruit i' the
country; for you'll be rotten ere you be half ripe, and
that's the right virtue of the medlar.

Touchstone. You have said; but whether wisely or no,
let the forest judge.   120

Enter CELIA, *reading a paper.*

Rosalind. Peace!
Here comes my sister, reading: stand aside.

Celia.   Why should this a desert be?
              For it is unpeopled? No;
          Tongues I'll hang on every tree,   125
              That shall civil sayings show.
          Some, how brief the life of man
              Runs his erring pilgrimage,
          That the stretching of a span
              Buckles in his sum of age;   130
          Some, of violated vows
              'Twixt the souls of friend and friend:
          But upon the fairest boughs,
              Or at every sentence' end,
          Will I Rosalinda write;   135
              Teaching all that read to know
          The quintessence of every sprite
              Heaven would in little show.
          Therefore Heaven Nature charg'd
              That one body should be fill'd   140
          With all graces wide enlarg'd:
              Nature presently distill'd

116 **medlar:** tree whose fruit is shaped like an apple, but flat
at the top, and only fit to be eaten when very ripe [*N*].   124
For: just because.   126 **civil sayings:** weighty sentences
[*N*].   128 **erring:** wandering.   129 **span:** space from the tip
of the thumb to the tip of the little finger when extended [*N*].
130 **buckles in:** embraces.   137 **The quintessence of every
sprite:** the refined perfection of every spirit, of every human
virtue [*N*].   138 **in little:** in mankind, or in miniature [*N*].
141 **wide enlarg'd:** spread abroad in various people.

Helen's cheek, but not her heart,
   Cleopatra's majesty,
Atalanta's better part,   145
   Sad Lucretia's modesty.
Thus Rosalind of many parts
   By heavenly synod was devis'd
Of many faces, eyes, and hearts,
   To have the touches dearest priz'd.   150
Heaven would that she these gifts should have,
And I to live and die her slave.

Rosalind. O most gentle Jupiter! what tedious homily of love have you wearied your parishioners withal, and never cried, 'Have patience, good people!'   155

Celia. How now! back, friends! Shepherd, go off a little: go with him, sirrah.

Touchstone. Come, shepherd, let us make an honourable retreat; though not with bag and baggage, yet with scrip and scrippage.   [*Exeunt* CORIN *and* TOUCHSTONE.

Celia. Didst thou hear these verses?   161

Rosalind. O, yes, I heard them all, and more too; for some of them had in them more feet than the verses would bear.   164

Celia. That's no matter: the feet might bear the verses.

Rosalind. Ay, but the feet were lame, and could not bear themselves without the verse, and therefore stood lamely in the verse.

Celia. But didst thou hear without wondering, how thy name should be hanged and carved upon these trees?   170

Rosalind. I was seven of the nine days out of the wonder before you came; for look here what I found on a palm-tree: I was never so be-rimed since Pythagoras' time, that I was an Irish rat, which I can hardly remember.

---

146 **Sad**: steadfast.   148 **synod**: council.   150 **touches**: traits.   154 **you**: i.e. Celia, or the author of the lines, *not* Jupiter. 159 **scrip**: wallet, pouch.   170 **should be**: could come to be. 173 **that**: when.

Celia. Trow you who hath done this?   **175**

Rosalind. Is it a man?

Celia. And a chain, that you once wore, about his neck.
Change you colour?

Rosalind. I prithee, who?   **179**

Celia. O Lord, Lord! it is a hard matter for friends to
meet; but mountains may be removed with earthquakes,
and so encounter.

Rosalind. Nay, but who is it?

Celia. Is it possible?   **184**

Rosalind. Nay, I prithee now, with most petitionary
vehemence, tell me who it is.

Celia. O wonderful, wonderful, and most wonderful
wonderful! and yet again wonderful! and after that, out
of all whooping!

Rosalind. Good my complexion! dost thou think, **190**
though I am caparison'd like a man, I have a doublet
and hose in my disposition? One inch of delay
more is a South-sea of discovery; I prithee, tell me
who is it quickly, and speak apace. I would thou
couldst stammer, that thou mightst pour this con- **195**
cealed man out of thy mouth, as wine comes out of a
narrow-mouth'd bottle; either too much at once, or
none at all. I prithee, take the cork out of thy mouth,
that I may drink thy tidings.

Celia. So you may put a man in your belly.   **200**

Rosalind. Is he of God's making? What manner of
man? Is his head worth a hat, or his chin worth a beard?

180–1 **friends to meet:** (i) make you understand me, or (ii) bring
you together (i.e. **friends** = lovers) [*N*].   184 **Is it possible?:**
i.e. that you do not know what I mean, or (perhaps) will not admit
that you know.   188–9 **out of all whooping:** beyond even a cry of
astonishment.   191–2 **I have . . . disposition:** i.e. my mind is
like a man's.   192–3 **One inch of delay more is a South-sea
of discovery:** one instant more of delay (in telling me) will plunge
me into endless conjecture [*N*].

Celia. Nay, he hath but a little beard.

Rosalind. Why, God will send more, if the man will be thankful. Let me stay the growth of his beard, if thou delay me not the knowledge of his chin.   206

Celia. It is young Orlando, that tripped up the wrestler's heels and your heart both, in an instant.

Rosalind. Nay, but the devil take mocking: speak, sad brow and true maid.   210

Celia. I' faith, coz, 'tis he،

Rosalind. Orlando?

Celia. Orlando.

Rosalind. Alas the day! what shall I do with my doublet and hose? What did he when thou sawest 215 him? What said he? How looked he? Wherein went he? What makes he here? Did he ask for me? Where remains he? How parted he with thee, and when shalt thou see him again? Answer me in one word.   219

Celia. You must borrow me Gargantua's mouth first: 'tis a word too great for any mouth of this age's size. To say ay and no to these particulars is more than to answer in a catechism.

Rosalind. But doth he know that I am in this forest and in man's apparel? Looks he as freshly as he did the day he wrestled?   226

Celia. It is as easy to count atomies as to resolve the propositions of a lover; but take a taste of my finding him, and relish it with good observance. I found him under a tree, like a dropped acorn.   230

---

205 **stay**: wait for.   209–10 **sad brow and true maid**: with a serious face and as a true maid, i.e. in all truth and seriousness. 216–17 **Wherein went he**: How was he dressed? 220 **Gargantua's mouth**: a giant's mouth [*N*].   227 **atomies**: motes in the sunbeams.   227–8 **resolve the propositions**: find the answer to the problems.   229 **relish it with good observance**: add the sauce of close attention to it.

Rosalind. It may well be called Jove's tree, when it drops forth such fruit.

Celia. Give me audience, good madam.

Rosalind. Proceed.   234

Celia. There lay he, stretch'd along like a wounded knight.

Rosalind. Though it be pity to see such a sight, it well becomes the ground.

Celia. Cry 'holla!' to thy tongue, I prithee; it curvets unseasonably. He was furnish'd like a hunter.   240

Rosalind. O, ominous! he comes to kill my heart.

Celia. I would sing my song without a burthen: thou bringest me out of tune.

Rosalind. Do you not know I am a woman? when I think, I must speak. Sweet, say on.   245

Celia. You bring me out. Soft! comes he not here?

Rosalind. 'Tis he: slink by, and note him.

Enter ORLANDO *and* JAQUES.

Jaques. I thank you for your company; but, good faith, I had as lief have been myself alone.

Orlando. And so had I; but yet, for fashion' sake, I thank you too for your society.   251

Jaques. God buy you: let's meet as little as we can.

Orlando. I do desire we may be better strangers.

Jaques. I pray you, mar no more trees with writing love-songs in their barks.   255

---

231 **Jove's tree:** the oak (sacred to Jove).   238 **ground:** earth, and also background.   239 **holla:** stop.   **curvets:** leaps with its four legs in the air (of a horse).   241 **heart:** a pun on 'heart' and 'hart'.   242 **burthen:** bass accompaniment.   246 **out:** out of tune, out of my stride (cf. l. 243).   249 **I had as lief:** I would have preferred.   252 **God buy you:** God be with you [N].   253 **better strangers:** a deliberate alteration of the usual better acquainted.

Orlando. I pray you mar no more of my verses with
reading them ill-favouredly.

Jaques. Rosalind is your love's name?

Orlando. Yes, just.

Jaques. I do not like her name.   260

Orlando. There was no thought of pleasing you when
she was christened.

Jaques. What stature is she of?

Orlando. Just as high as my heart.   264

Jaques. You are full of pretty answers. Have you not
been acquainted with goldsmiths' wives, and conn'd them
out of rings?

Orlando. Not so; but I answer you right painted cloth,
from whence you have studied your questions.   269

Jaques. You have a nimble wit: I think 'twas made of
Atalanta's heels. Will you sit down with me? and we two
will rail against our mistress the world, and all our misery.

Orlando. I will chide no breather in the world but myself,
against whom I know most faults.

Jaques. The worst fault you have is to be in love.   275

Orlando. 'Tis a fault I will not change for your best
virtue. I am weary of you.

Jaques. By my troth, I was seeking for a fool when I
found you.   279

Orlando. He is drowned in the brook: look but in, and
you shall see him.

Jaques. There I shall see mine own figure.

Orlando. Which I take to be either a fool or a cipher.

Jaques. I'll tarry no longer with you. Farewell, good
Signior Love.   285

Orlando. I am glad of your departure. Adieu, good
Monsieur Melancholy.   [*Exit* JAQUES.

---

259 **just:** exactly so.   266 **conn'd:** learned [*N*].   268 **right
painted cloth:** with true brevity [*N*].   273 **breather:** living
person.   283 **cipher:** the figure 0.

Rosalind. I will speak to him like a saucy lackey, and under that habit play the knave with him. Do you hear, forester?   290

Orlando. Very well: what would you?

Rosalind. I pray you, what is't o'clock?

Orlando. You should ask me, what time o' day; there's no clock in the forest.   294

Rosalind. Then there is no true lover in the forest; else sighing every minute and groaning every hour would detect the lazy foot of Time as well as a clock.

Orlando. And why not the swift foot of Time? had not that been as proper?   299

Rosalind. By no means, sir. Time travels in divers paces with divers persons. I'll tell you who Time ambles withal, who Time trots withal, who Time gallops withal, and who he stands still withal.

Orlando. I prithee, who doth he trot withal?   304

Rosalind. Marry, he trots hard with a young maid between the contract of her marriage and the day it is solemnized; if the interim be but a se'nnight, Time's pace is so hard that it seems the length of seven year.

Orlando. Who ambles Time withal?   309

Rosalind. With a priest that lacks Latin, and a rich man that hath not the gout; for the one sleeps easily because he cannot study, and the other lives merrily because he feels no pain; the one lacking the burden of lean and wasteful learning, the other knowing no burden of heavy tedious penury. These Time ambles withal. 315

Orlando. Who doth he gallop withal?

Rosalind. With a thief to the gallows; for though he go as softly as foot can fall he thinks himself too soon there.

Orlando. Who stays it still withal?   319

---

289 **under that habit**: in that guise.   297 **detect**: find out.
302 **who ... withal**: with whom.   305 **hard**: at an uneasy
pace [*N*].

Rosalind. With lawyers in the vacation; for they sleep
between term and term, and then they perceive not how
Time moves.

Orlando. Where dwell you, pretty youth?

Rosalind. With this shepherdess, my sister; here in the
skirts of the forest, like fringe upon a petticoat.   325

Orlando. Are you native of this place?

Rosalind. As the cony, that you see dwell where she is
kindled.

Orlando. Your accent is something finer than you could
purchase in so removed a dwelling.   330

Rosalind. I have been told so of many: but indeed
an old religious uncle of mine taught me to speak, who
was in his youth an inland man; one that knew courtship too well, for there he fell in love. I have heard him
read many lectures against it; and I thank God, I am 335
not a woman, to be touched with so many giddy
offences as he hath generally taxed their whole sex
withal.

Orlando. Can you remember any of the principal evils
that he laid to the charge of women?   340

Rosalind. There were none principal; they were all like
one another as half-pence are; every one fault seeming
monstrous till his fellow fault came to match it.

Orlando. I prithee, recount some of them.

Rosalind. No, I will not cast away my physic, but on 345
those that are sick. There is a man haunts the forest,
that abuses our young plants with carving 'Rosalind'
on their barks; hangs odes upon hawthorns, and elegies

---

326 **native of**: native to.   327 **cony**: rabbit.   328 **kindled**:
born, especially of the rabbit.   330 **purchase**: acquire.   331
of: by.   332 **religious**: member of a religious order.   333
inland: cf. Act II, sc. vii, l. 96 and footnote.   333 **courtship**:
(i) life of courts, (ii) wooing.   336 **touched**: tainted.   337
generally: speaking of them as a class.   343 **his**: its.

on brambles; all, forsooth, deifying the name of
Rosalind: if I could meet that fancy-monger, I would 350
give him some good counsel, for he seems to have the
quotidian of love upon him.

Orlando. I am he that is so love-shaked. I pray you, tell
me your remedy.   354

Rosalind. There is none of my uncle's marks upon you:
he taught me how to know a man in love; in which cage
of rushes I am sure you are not prisoner.

Orlando. What were his marks?

Rosalind. A lean cheek, which you have not; a blue
eye and sunken, which you have not; an unquestionable 360
spirit, which you have not; a beard neglected, which
you have not: but I pardon you for that, for, simply,
your having in beard is a younger brother's revenue.
Then, your hose should be ungartered, your bonnet
unbanded, your sleeve unbuttoned, your shoe untied, 365
and everything about you demonstrating a careless
desolation. But you are no such man: you are rather
point-device in your accoutrements; as loving yourself
than seeming the lover of any other.

Orlando. Fair youth, I would I could make thee believe
I love.   371

Rosalind. Me believe it! you may as soon make her
that you love believe it; which, I warrant, she is apter
to do than to confess she does; that is one of the points
in the which women still give the lie to their consciences. 375

---

350 **fancy-monger:** dealer in love.   352 **quotidian:** daily, i.e.
constant fever [*N*].   353 **love-shaked:** in an ague because of
love.   359–60 **blue eye:** hollow eye, with dark circles round it.
360 **unquestionable:** unwilling to talk and be questioned.
362–3 **simply . . . revenue:** indeed, the amount of beard you have
is small like a younger brother's allowance.   365 **unbanded:**
without a hat-band.   368 **point-device:** particular to the point
of being finicky [*N*].   375 **still:** always.   **give the lie to:**
deceive.

But, in good sooth, are you he that hangs the verses on
the trees, wherein Rosalind is so admired?

Orlando. I swear to thee, youth, by the white hand of
Rosalind, I am that he, that unfortunate he.

Rosalind. But are you so much in love as your rimes
speak? 381

Orlando. Neither rime nor reason can express how much.

Rosalind. Love is merely a madness, and, I tell you,
deserves as well a dark house and a whip as madmen do;
and the reason why they are not so punished and cured is,
that the lunacy is so ordinary that the whippers are in
love too. Yet I profess curing it by counsel.

Orlando. Did you ever cure any so?

Rosalind. Yes, one; and in this manner. He was to
imagine me his love, his mistress; and I set him every 390
day to woo me: at which time would I, being but a
moonish youth, grieve, be effeminate, changeable, longing and liking; proud, fantastical, apish, shallow, incon-
stant, full of tears, full of smiles, for every passion
something, and for no passion truly anything, as boys 395
and women are, for the most part, cattle of this colour;
would now like him, now loathe him; then entertain
him, then forswear him; now weep for him, then spit at
him; that I drave my suitor from his mad humour of
love to a living humour of madness, which was, to 400
forswear the full stream of the world, and to live in a
nook merely monastic. And thus I cured him; and this
way will I take upon me to wash your liver as clean as a
sound sheep's heart, that there shall not be one spot of
love in 't. 405

383 **merely**: altogether, purely.   392 **moonish**: changeable,
like the moon.   393 **apish**: affected, foolishly imitative.   394–5
for every passion . . . anything: affecting the symptoms of every
emotion, but none of them genuine.   396 **cattle of this colour**:
beings of the nature described.   398 **forswear**: refuse.   400
living: real, actual.

Orlando. I would not be cured, youth.

Rosalind. I would cure you, if you would but call me
Rosalind, and come every day to my cote and woo me.

Orlando. Now, by the faith of my love, I will: tell me
where it is. 410

Rosalind. Go with me to it and I'll show it you; and by
the way you shall tell me where in the forest you live.
Will you go?

Orlando. With all my heart, good youth. 414

Rosalind. Nay, you must call me Rosalind. Come, sister,
will you go? [*Exeunt.*

Scene III. ANOTHER PART OF THE FOREST

Enter TOUCHSTONE *and* AUDREY; JAQUES *behind.*

Touchstone. Come apace, good Audrey: I will fetch up
your goats, Audrey. And how, Audrey? am I the man
yet? doth my simple feature content you? 3

Audrey. Your features! Lord warrant us! what features?

Touchstone. I am here with thee and thy goats, as the
most capricious poet, honest Ovid, was among the Goths.

Jaques. [*Aside.*] O knowledge ill-inhabited, worse than
Jove in a thatch'd house! 8

Touchstone. When a man's verses cannot be understood,
nor a man's good wit seconded with the forward child
understanding, it strikes a man more dead than a great
reckoning in a little room. Truly, I would the gods had
made thee poetical.

Audrey. I do not know what 'poetical' is. Is it honest
in deed and word? Is it a true thing? 15

Touchstone. No, truly, for the truest poetry is the most

3 feature: general form.   **6 capricious:** fanciful [*N*].   **7
ill-inhabited:** ill-lodged.   **11–12 a great reckoning in a little
room:** a huge hotel bill in a small tavern-room [*N*].   **14 honest:**
chaste.

feigning; and lovers are given to poetry, and what they
swear in poetry may be said as lovers they do feign.

Audrey. Do you wish then that the gods had made me
poetical?   20

Touchstone. I do, truly; for thou swearest to me thou art
honest: now, if thou wert a poet, I might have some hope
thou didst feign.

Audrey. Would you not have me honest?   24

Touchstone. No, truly, unless thou wert hard-favour'd;
for honesty coupled to beauty is to have honey a sauce to
sugar.

Jaques. [*Aside.*] A material fool. *A fool full of ideas; someone who has no ideas.*

Audrey. Well, I am not fair, and therefore I pray the
gods make me honest.   30

Touchstone. Truly, and to cast away honesty upon a foul
slut were to put good meat into an unclean dish.

Audrey. I am not a slut, though I thank the gods I am
foul.   34

Touchstone. Well, praised be the gods for thy foulness!
sluttishness may come hereafter. But be it as it may be,
I will marry thee; and to that end I have been with Sir
Oliver Martext, the vicar of the next village, who hath
promised to meet me in this place of the forest, and to
couple us.   40

Jaques. [*Aside.*] I would fain see this meeting.

Audrey. Well, the gods give us joy!

Touchstone. Amen. A man may, if he were of a fearful
heart, stagger in this attempt; for here we have no
temple but the wood, no assembly but horn-beasts. 45
But what though? Courage! As horns are odious, they

17–18 what they swear ... feign: it may be said that, as lovers,
they do not carry out what they vow to do in poetry, i.e. they
cannot be trusted as lovers.   **26–7 honey ... sugar:** i.e. too much
of a good thing.   **28 material:** full of ideas.   **31 foul:** homely,
not fair (cf. l. 29).   **44 stagger:** hesitate.

are necessary. It is said, 'many a man knows no end of
his goods:' right; many a man has good horns, and
knows no end of them. Well, that is the dowry of his
wife; 'tis none of his own getting. Horns? Even so. 50
Poor men alone? No, no; the noblest deer hath them
as huge as the rascal. Is the single man therefore
blessed? No: as a walled town is more worthier than a
village, so is the forehead of a married man more
honourable than the bare brow of a bachelor; and by 55
how much defence is better than no skill, by so much is
a horn more precious than to want. Here comes Sir
Oliver.

Enter SIR OLIVER MARTEXT. *of wisdom — another remarks from Touchstone*

Sir Oliver Martext, you are well met: will you dispatch
us here under this tree, or shall we go with you to your
chapel?   61
  Sir Oliver. Is there none here to give the woman?
  Touchstone. I will not take her on gift of any man.
  Sir Oliver. Truly, she must be given, or the marriage is
not lawful.   65
  Jaques. [*Coming forward.*] Proceed, proceed: I'll give her.
  Touchstone. Good even, good Master What-ye-call't:
how do you, sir? You are very well met: God 'ild you for
your last company: I am very glad to see you: even a
toy in hand here, sir: nay, pray be covered.   70
  Jaques. Will you be married, motley?
  Touchstone. As the ox hath his bow, sir, the horse his

---

47 necessary: unavoidable [*N*].   **49 dowry:** what he gets along
with his wife.   **51 Poor men alone?:** do only poor men have
them?   **52 rascal:** young, lean, or inferior deer, distinguished
from the full-grown antlered bucks or stags (*O.E.D.*).   **56 defence:**
the art of fencing.   **57 a horn . . . want:** an unfaithful wife
better than none.   **68 God 'ild you:** God repay you.   **70 toy
in hand:** mere trifle, i.e. Audrey.   **be covered:** put on your
hat [*N*].   **72 bow:** yoke.

curb, and the falcon her bells, so man hath his desires; and as pigeons bill, so wedlock would be nibbling.

Jaques. And will you, being a man of your breeding, 75 be married under a bush, like a beggar? Get you to church, and have a good priest that can tell you what marriage is: this fellow will but join you together as they join wainscot; then one of you will prove a shrunk panel, and like green timber, warp, warp. 80

Touchstone. [*Aside.*] I am not in the mind but I were better to be married of him than of another: for he is not like to marry me well, and not being well married, it will be a good excuse for me hereafter to leave my wife.

Jaques. Go thou with me, and let me counsel thee. 85

Touchstone. Come, sweet Audrey:
We must be married, or we must live in bawdry.
Farewell, good Master Oliver: not

> O sweet Oliver!
> O brave Oliver! 90
> Leave me not behind thee:

but,—

> Wind away,
> Begone, I say,
> I will not to wedding with thee. 95

[*Exeunt* JAQUES, TOUCHSTONE, *and* AUDREY.

Sir Oliver. 'Tis no matter: ne'er a fantastical knave of them all shall flout me out of my calling. [*Exit.*

Scene IV. ANOTHER PART OF THE FOREST

Enter ROSALIND *and* CELIA.

Rosalind. Never talk to me: I will weep.

---

74 bill: caress one another (with their bills). **80 green:** unseasoned. **81-2 I am not in the mind . . . another:** I am in no other mind than that it would be better to be married by him than by another (**but** = except). **87 bawdry:** dishonesty, unchastity.

Celia. Do, I prithee; but yet have the grace to consider that tears do not become a man.

Rosalind. But have I not cause to weep?   4

Celia. As good cause as one would desire; therefore weep.

Rosalind. His very hair is of the dissembling colour.

Celia. Something browner than Judas's; marry, his kisses are Judas's own children.

Rosalind. I' faith, his hair is of a good colour.   10

Celia. An excellent colour: your chestnut was ever the only colour.

Rosalind. And his kissing is as full of sanctity as the touch of holy bread.   14

Celia. He hath bought a pair of cast lips of Diana: a nun of winter's sisterhood kisses not more religiously; the very ice of chastity is in them.

Rosalind. But why did he swear he would come this morning, and comes not?

Celia. Nay, certainly, there is no truth in him.   20

Rosalind. Do you think so?

Celia. Yes: I think he is not a pick-purse nor a horse-stealer; but for his verity in love, I do think him as concave as a covered goblet or a worm-eaten nut.

Rosalind. Not true in love?   25

Celia. Yes, when he is in; but I think he is not in.

Rosalind. You have heard him swear downright he was.

Celia. 'Was' is not 'is': besides, the oath of a lover is no stronger than the word of a tapster; they are both the confirmers of false reckonings. He attends here in the forest on the duke your father.   31

Rosalind. I met the duke yesterday and had much

---

7 dissembling: deceitful.   **14 holy bread:** sacramental wafer.
15 cast: cast-off.   **Diana:** goddess of chastity.   **24 concave as a covered goblet:** hollow as the inside of a goblet when its cover is on [*N*].   **30 confirmers of:** ready to affirm, swear to.

question with him. He asked me of what parentage I was;
I told him, of as good as he; so he laughed, and let me go.
But what talk we of fathers, when there is such a man as
Orlando?   36

Celia. O, that's a brave man! he writes brave verses,
speaks brave words, swears brave oaths, and breaks
them bravely, quite traverse, athwart the heart of his
lover; as a puisny tilter, that spurs his horse but on one   40
side, breaks his staff like a noble goose. But all's brave
that youth mounts and folly guides. Who comes here?

Enter CORIN.

Corin. Mistress and master, you have oft inquir'd
After the shepherd that complain'd of love,
Who you saw sitting by me on the turf,   45
Praising the proud disdainful shepherdess
That was his mistress.

Celia.   Well, and what of him?

Corin. If you will see a pageant truly play'd,
Between the pale complexion of true love
And the red glow of scorn and proud disdain,   50
Go hence a little, and I shall conduct you,
If you will mark it.

Rosalind.   O! come, let us remove:
The sight of lovers feedeth those in love.
Bring us to this sight, and you shall say   54
I'll prove a busy actor in their play.   [*Exeunt.*

Scene V. ANOTHER PART OF THE FOREST

Enter SILVIUS *and* PHEBE.

Silvius. Sweet Phebe, do not scorn me; do not, Phebe:
Say that you love me not, but say not so

33 **question:** talk.   35 **what:** why.   37 **brave:** fine, gallant
(ironic).   39 **traverse:** crosswise, not straight (like the glancing
thrust of a sword) [*N*].   40 **lover:** beloved.   **puisny:** junior,
and so young and inexperienced.

In bitterness. The common executioner,
Whose heart the accustom'd sight of death makes hard,
Falls not the axe upon the humbled neck   5
But first begs pardon: will you sterner be
Than he that dies and lives by bloody drops?

     Enter ROSALIND, CELIA, *and* CORIN, *behind.*

  Phebe. I would not be thy executioner:
I fly thee, for I would not injure thee.
Thou tell'st me there is murder in mine eye: 10
'Tis pretty, sure, and very probable,
That eyes, that are the frail'st and softest things,
Who shut their coward gates on atomies,
Should be call'd tyrants, butchers, murderers!
Now I do frown on thee with all my heart;   15
And, if mine eyes can wound, now let them kill thee;
Now counterfeit to swound; why, now fall down;
Or, if thou canst not, O! for shame, for shame,
Lie not, to say mine eyes are murderers.
Now show the wound mine eye hath made in thee;   20
Scratch thee but with a pin, and there remains
Some scar of it; lean but upon a rush,
The cicatrice and capable impressure
Thy palm some moment keeps; but now mine eyes,
Which I have darted at thee, hurt thee not,   25
Nor, I am sure, there is no force in eyes
That can do hurt.
  Silvius.   O dear Phebe,
If ever,—as that ever may be near,—
You meet in some fresh cheek the power of fancy,

---

5 **Falls**: lets fall (i.e. transitive).   7 **dies and lives**: subsists
throughout his whole life [*N*].   11 **sure**: surely (sarcastic).
13 **atomies**: motes.   17 **swound**: swoon.   19 **Lie not, to say**:
do not lie by saying.   23 **cicatrice**: here merely mark, not scar.
capable impressure: retentive impression, i.e. one able to be
retained.   29 **power of fancy**: power to excite your love.

Then shall you know the wounds invisible   80
That love's keen arrows make.
   Phebe.   But, till that time
Come not thou near me; and, when that time comes,
Afflict me with thy mocks, pity me not;
As, till that time I shall not pity thee.
   Rosalind. [*Advancing.*] And why, I pray you? Who
     might be your mother,   85
That you insult, exult, and all at once,
Over the wretched? What though you have no beauty,—
As by my faith, I see no more in you
Than without candle may go dark to bed,—
Must you be therefore proud and pitiless?   40
Why, what means this? Why do you look on me?
I see no more in you than in the ordinary
Of nature's sale-work. Od's my little life!
I think she means to tangle my eyes too.
No, faith, proud mistress, hope not after it: 45
'Tis not your inky brows, your black silk hair,
Your bugle eyeballs, nor your cheek of cream,
That can entame my spirits to your worship.
You foolish shepherd, wherefore do you follow her;
Like foggy south puffing with wind and rain?   50
You are a thousand times a properer man
Than she a woman: 'tis such fools as you
That make the world full of ill-favour'd children:
'Tis not her glass, but you, that flatters her;
And out of you she sees herself more proper   55
Than any of her lineaments can show her.

---

35 **Who might be your mother:** i.e. who are you to insult the
wretched?   42–3 **the ordinary of nature's sale-work:** the usual
run of nature's ready-made goods, goods made to stock pattern.
47 **bugle:** black, like beads.   48 **entame:** make tame.   50
Like . . . south: like a fog-bearing south wind [*N*].   51 **properer:** handsomer.   55 **out of you:** in your eyes.

But, mistress, know yourself: down on your knees,
And thank heaven, fasting, for a good man's love:
For I must tell you friendly in your ear,
Sell when you can; you are not for all markets. 60
Cry the man mercy; love him; take his offer:
Foul is most foul, being foul to be a scoffer.
So take her to thee, shepherd. Fare you well.

Phebe. Sweet youth, I pray you, chide a year together:
I had rather hear you chide than this man woo. 65

Rosalind. He's fallen in love with your foulness, and
she'll fall in love with my anger. If it be so, as fast as she
answers thee with frowning looks, I'll sauce her with bitter
words. Why look you so upon me?

Phebe. For no ill will I bear you. 70

Rosalind. I pray you, do not fall in love with me,
For I am falser than vows made in wine:
Besides, I like you not. If you will know my house,
'Tis at the tuft of olives here hard by.
Will you go, sister? Shepherd, ply her hard. 75
Come, sister. Shepherdess, look on him better,
And be not proud: though all the world could see,
None could be so abus'd in sight as he.
Come, to our flock. [*Exeunt* ROSALIND, CELIA, *and* CORIN.

Phebe. Dead shepherd, now I find thy saw of might: 80
'Who ever lov'd that lov'd not at first sight?'

Silvius. Sweet Phebe,—

Phebe.   Ha! what sayst thou, Silvius?

Silvius. Sweet Phebe, pity me.

Phebe. Why, I am sorry for thee, gentle Silvius.

---

61 **Cry the man mercy:** ask the man for mercy.   62 **Foul ...
scoffer:** the worst form of ugliness (both moral and physical) is
for one who is ugly to be also cruelly disdainful.   77–8 **though
all the world . . . in sight as he:** 'though all mankind could look
on you, none could be so deceived as to think you beautiful but he'
(Dr. Johnson).

Silvius. Wherever sorrow is, relief would be: 85
If you do sorrow at my grief in love,
By giving love your sorrow and my grief
Were both extermin'd.
  Phebe. Thou hast my love: is not that neighbourly?
  Silvius. I would have you.
  Phebe.   Why, that were covetousness.
Silvius, the time was that I hated thee;   91
And yet it is not that I bear thee love:
But since that thou canst talk of love so well,
Thy company, which erst was irksome to me,
I will endure, and I'll employ thee too;   95
But do not look for further recompense
Than thine own gladness that thou art employ'd,
  Silvius. So holy and so perfect is my love,
And I in such a poverty of grace,
That I shall think it a most plenteous crop   100
To glean the broken ears after the man
That the main harvest reaps: loose now and then
A scatter'd smile, and that I'll live upon.
  Phebe. Know'st thou the youth that spoke to me erewhile?
  Silvius. Not very well, but I have met him oft;   105
And he hath bought the cottage and the bounds
That the old carlot once was master of.
  Phebe. Think not I love him, though I ask for him,
'Tis but a peevish boy; yet he talks well;
But what care I for words? yet words do well,   110
When he that speaks them pleases those that hear.
It is a pretty youth: not very pretty:
But, sure, he's proud; and yet his pride becomes him:
He'll make a proper man: the best thing in him

88 **extermin'd**: exterminated.   94 **erst**: before.   99 **in
such a poverty of grace**: so little graciousness has been shown me
(by you).   102 **That . . . reaps**: who reaps the main harvest (of
your love).   107 **carlot**: churl, peasant.

Is his complexion; and faster than his tongue   115
Did make offence his eye did heal it up.
He is not very tall; yet for his years he's tall;
His leg is but so so; and yet 'tis well:
There was a pretty redness in his lip,
A little riper and more lusty red   120
Than that mix'd in his cheek; 'twas just the difference
Betwixt the constant red and mingled damask.
There be some women, Silvius, had they mark'd him
In parcels as I did, would have gone near
To fall in love with him; but, for my part,   125
I love him not nor hate him not; and yet
Have more cause to hate him than to love him:
For what had he to do to chide at me?
He said mine eyes were black and my hair black;
And, now I am remember'd, scorn'd at me.   130
I marvel why I answer'd not again:
But that's all one; omittance is no quittance,
I'll write to him a very taunting letter,
And thou shalt bear it: wilt thou, Silvius?
  Silvius. Phebe, with all my heart.
  Phebe.   I'll write it straight;
The matter's in my head and in my heart: 136
I will be bitter with him and passing short.
Go with me, Silvius.   [*Exeunt.*

122 **mingled damask:** a mixture of red and white, like damask
roses [*N*].   124 **parcels:** particular details.   128 **what . . .
do:** what business had he.   130 **I am remember'd:** I remember.
132 **omittance is no quittance:** to ignore is not to acquit.
137 **passing:** very.

ACT IV

Scene I. The Forest of Arden

Enter ROSALIND, CELIA, *and* JAQUES.

Jaques. I prithee, pretty youth, let me be better acquainted with thee.

Rosalind. They say you are a melancholy fellow.

Jaques. I am so; I do love it better than laughing. **4**

Rosalind. Those that are in extremity of either are abominable fellows, and betray themselves to every modern censure worse than drunkards.

Jaques. Why, 'tis good to be sad and say nothing.

Rosalind. Why, then, 'tis good to be a post.

Jaques. I have neither the scholar's melancholy, **10** which is emulation; nor the musician's, which is fantastical; nor the courtier's, which is proud; nor the soldier's, which is ambitious; nor the lawyer's, which is politic; nor the lady's, which is nice; nor the lover's, which is all these: but it is a melancholy of mine own, **15** compounded of many simples, extracted from many objects, and indeed the sundry contemplation of my travels, in which my often rumination wraps me in a most humorous sadness. **19**

Rosalind. A traveller! By my faith, you have great reason to be sad. I fear you have sold your own lands to see other men's; then, to have seen much and to have nothing, is to have rich eyes and poor hands.

Jaques. Yes, I have gained my experience. **24**

Rosalind. And your experience makes you sad: I had

---

7 modern: commonplace.　　**11 emulation:** jealousy, rivalry (of other scholars).　　**12 fantastical:** fanciful, or emotional. **14 politic:** diplomatic, a matter of policy.　　**nice:** trifling and fastidious.　　**16 simples:** ingredients (in medicine, usually herbs).

rather have a fool to make me merry than experience to make me sad: and to travel for it too!

Enter ORLANDO.

Orlando. Good day, and happiness, dear Rosalind!

Jaques. Nay then, God buy you, an you talk in blank verse.   [*Exit.*

Rosalind. Farewell, Monsieur Traveller: look you lisp, 31 and wear strange suits, disable all the benefits of your own country, be out of love with your nativity, and almost chide God for making you that countenance you are; or I will scarce think you have swam in a 35 gondola. Why, how now, Orlando! where have you been all this while? You a lover! An you serve me such another trick, never come in my sight more.

Orlando. My fair Rosalind, I come within an hour of my promise.   40

Rosalind. Break an hour's promise in love! He that will divide a minute into a thousand parts, and break but a part of the thousandth part of a minute in the affairs of love, it may be said of him that Cupid hath clapped him o' the shoulder, but I'll warrant him heart-whole.   45

Orlando. Pardon me, dear Rosalind.

Rosalind. Nay, an you be so tardy, come no more in my sight: I had as lief be wooed of a snail.

Orlando. Of a snail!   49

Rosalind. Ay, of a snail; for though he comes slowly, he carries his house on his head; a better jointure, I think, than you make a woman: besides, he brings his destiny with him.

Orlando. What's that?   54

---

30 **an:** if.   32 **disable:** undervalue.   35–6 **swam in a gondola:** i.e. been in Italy.   44–5 **clapp'd him o' the shoulder:** (i) given him a friendly slap, or (ii) arrested him.   51 **jointure:** marriage settlement.

Rosalind. Why, horns; that such as you are fain to be beholding to your wives for: but he comes armed in his fortune and prevents the slander of his wife.

Orlando. Virtue is no horn-maker; and my Rosalind is virtuous.

Rosalind. And I am your Rosalind? 60

Celia. It pleases him to call you so; but he hath a Rosalind of a better leer than you.

Rosalind. Come, woo me, woo me; for now I am in a holiday humour, and like enough to consent. What would you say to me now, an I were your very very Rosalind? 65

Orlando. I would kiss before I spoke.

Rosalind. Nay, you were better speak first, and when you were gravelled for lack of matter, you might take occasion to kiss. Very good orators, when they are out, they will spit; and for lovers lacking,—God warn us!— matter, the cleanliest shift is to kiss. 71

Orlando. How if the kiss be denied?

Rosalind. Then she puts you to entreaty, and there begins new matter.

Orlando. Who could be out, being before his beloved mistress? 76

Rosalind. Marry, that should you, if I were your mistress; or I should think my honesty ranker than my wit.

Orlando. What, of my suit?

Rosalind. Not out of your apparel, and yet out of your suit. Am not I your Rosalind? 81

---

56 beholding: indebted (beholden). **56–7 he comes ... fortune:** he already has what it is his fortune to get later (by marriage). **57 prevents:** anticipates. **62 leer:** face, complexion. **68 gravelled:** stuck (like a ship in sand). **69 are out:** have nothing to say. **70 God warn us:** Mercy on us! (**warn** = warrant), i.e. is such a thing possible! **71 shift:** expedient. **78 I should ... wit:** i.e. I shouldn't think much of my wits if I couldn't silence you (**ranker** = stronger, of richer growth).

Orlando. I take some joy to say you are, because I would
be talking of her.

Rosalind. Well, in her person I say I will not have you.

Orlando. Then in mine own person I die.   85

Rosalind. No, faith, die by attorney. The poor world
is almost six thousand years old, and in all this time
there was not any man died in his own person, *videlicet,*
in a love-cause. Troilus had his brains dashed out with
a Grecian club; yet he did what he could to die before,   90
and he is one of the patterns of love. Leander, he would
have lived many a fair year, though Hero had turned
nun, if it had not been for a hot midsummer night;
for, good youth, he went but forth to wash him in the
Hellespont, and being taken with the cramp was   95
drowned; and the foolish chroniclers of that age
found it was Hero of Sestos. But these are all lies: men
have died from time to time, and worms have eaten
them, but not for love.

Orlando. I would not have my right Rosalind of this
mind; for, I protest, her frown might kill me.   101

Rosalind. By this hand, it will not kill a fly. But come,
now I will be your Rosalind in a more coming-on disposition; and ask me what you will, I will grant it.

Orlando. Then love me, Rosalind.   105

Rosalind. Yes, faith will I, Fridays and Saturdays
and all.

Orlando. And wilt thou have me?

Rosalind. Ay, and twenty such,

Orlando. What sayest thou?   110

Rosalind. Are you not good?

Orlando. I hope so.

---

86 die by attorney: authorize some one to die on your behalf,
i.e. not in your own person.   **88 *videlicet*:** that is to say.   **97**
found it was Hero: decided that Hero was the cause.   **100**
right: true, real.   **103 coming-on:** encouraging.

Rosalind. Why then, can one desire too much of a good thing?—Come, sister, you shall be the priest and marry us.—Give me your hand, Orlando. What do you say, sister? 106

Orlando. Pray thee, marry us.

Celia. I cannot say the words.

Rosalind. You must begin,—'Will you, Orlando,'—

Celia. Go to.—Will you, Orlando, have to wife this Rosalind? 111

Orlando. I will.

Rosalind. Ay, but when?

Orlando. Why now; as fast as she can marry us.

Rosalind. Then you must say, 'I take thee, Rosalind, for wife.' 116

Orlando. I take thee, Rosalind, for wife.

Rosalind. I might ask you for your commission; but, I do take thee, Orlando, for my husband: there's a girl goes before the priest; and, certainly, a woman's thought runs before her actions. 121

Orlando. So do all thoughts; they are winged.

Rosalind. Now tell me how long you would have her after you have possessed her?

Orlando. For ever and a day. 125

Rosalind. Say 'a day,' without the 'ever.' No, no, Orlando; men are April when they woo, December when they wed: maids are May when they are maids, but the sky changes when they are wives. I will be more jealous of thee than a Barbary cock-pigeon over 130 his hen; more clamorous than a parrot against rain; more new-fangled than an ape; more giddy in my desires than a monkey: I will weep for nothing, like Diana in the fountain, and I will do that when you are disposed

---

118 **commission**: authority, i.e. to take her as wife, with nobody to give her away. 119–20 **goes before**: anticipates. 131 **against**: before. 132 **new-fangled**: fond of novelty [N].

to be merry; I will laugh like a hyen, and that when 135
thou art inclined to sleep.

Orlando. But will my Rosalind do so?

Rosalind. By my life, she will do as I do.

Orlando. O! but she is wise.   139

Rosalind. Or else she could not have the wit to do this:
the wiser, the waywarder: make the doors upon a woman's
wit, and it will out at the casement; shut that, and 'twill
out at the key-hole; stop that, 'twill fly with the smoke out
at the chimney.   144

Orlando. A man that had a wife with such a wit, he
might say, 'Wit, whither wilt?'

Rosalind. Nay, you might keep that check for it till you
met your wife's wit going to your neighbour's bed.   148

Orlando. And what wit could wit have to excuse that?

Rosalind. Marry, to say she came to seek you there.
You shall never take her without her answer, unless you
take her without her tongue. O! that woman that cannot
make her fault her husband's occasion, let her never nurse
her child herself, for she will breed it like a fool.

Orlando. For these two hours, Rosalind, I will leave
thee.   156

Rosalind. Alas! dear love, I cannot lack thee two hours.

Orlando. I must attend the duke at dinner: by two
o'clock I will be with thee again.   159

Rosalind. Ay, go your ways, go your ways; I knew what
you would prove, my friends told me as much, and I
thought no less: that flattering tongue of yours won me:
'tis but one cast away, and so, come, death! Two o'clock
is your hour?

Orlando. Ay, sweet Rosalind.   165

Rosalind. By my troth, and in good earnest, and so

---

135 **hyen:** hyena [*N*].   141 **make:** bar.   153 **husband's
occasion:** handle against her husband, i.e. opportunity to get the
better of him.   163 **one:** one heart, one person [*N*].

God mend me, and by all pretty oaths that are not
dangerous, if you break one jot of your promise or
come one minute behind your hour, I will think you the
most pathetical break-promise, and the most hollow 170
lover, and the most unworthy of her you call Rosalind,
that may be chosen out of the gross band of the unfaithful. Therefore, beware my censure, and keep your
promise.   174

Orlando. With no less religion than if thou wert indeed
my Rosalind: so, adieu.

Rosalind. Well, Time is the old justice that examines
all such offenders, and let Time try. Adieu.   178

                                          [*Exit* ORLANDO.

Celia. You have simply misused our sex in your love-
prate: we must have your doublet and hose plucked over
your head, and show the world what the bird hath done
to her own nest.   182

Rosalind. O coz, coz, coz, my pretty little coz, that thou
didst know how many fathom deep I am in love! But it
cannot be sounded: my affection hath an unknown bottom,
like the bay of Portugal.   186

Celia. Or rather, bottomless; that as fast as you pour
affection in, it runs out.

Rosalind. No; that same wicked bastard of Venus,
that was begot of thought, conceived of spleen, and 190
born of madness, that blind rascally boy that abuses
every one's eyes because his own are out, let him be
judge how deep I am in love. I'll tell thee, Aliena, I
cannot be out of the sight of Orlando: I'll go find a
shadow and sigh till he come.   195

Celia. And I'll sleep.   [*Exeunt.*

---

170 **pathetical:** pitiful [*N*].   172 **gross:** (i) total and (ii) enor-
mous.   179 **simply:** utterly, absolutely.   189 **wicked bastard:** i.e. Cupid.   190 **thought:** melancholy [*N*].   **spleen:**
passionate impulse [*N*].   195 **shadow:** shady spot.

Scene II. ANOTHER PART OF THE FOREST

Enter JAQUES, Lords, *and* Foresters,

Jaques. Which is he that killed the deer?

First Lord. Sir, it was I.

Jaques. Let's present him to the duke, like a Roman conqueror; and it would do well to set the deer's horns upon his head for a branch of victory. Have you no song, forester, for this purpose? 6

Second Lord. Yes, sir.

Jaques. Sing it: 'tis no matter how it be in tune so it make noise enough.

SONG

What shall he have that kill'd the deer? 10
His leather skin and horns to wear.
    Then sing him home.
                    [*The rest shall bear this burden.*
Take thou no scorn to wear the horn;
It was a crest ere thou wast born:
        Thy father's father wore it, 15
        And thy father bore it:
The horn, the horn, the lusty horn
Is not a thing to laugh to scorn.

Exeunt.

Scene III. ANOTHER PART OF THE FOREST

Enter ROSALIND *and* CELIA.

Rosalind. How say you now? Is it not past two o'clock? And here much Orlando!

Celia. I warrant you, with pure love and troubled brain, he hath ta'en his bow and arrows, and is gone forth to sleep. Look, who comes here. 5

12 (*s.d.*) **burden:** chorus. 4–5 **he hath ta'en . . . sleep:** i.e. went out to hunt but fell asleep instead.

Enter SILVIUS.

Silvius. My errand is to you, fair youth.
My gentle Phebe did bid me give you this: [*Giving a letter.*
I know not the contents; but, as I guess
By the stern brow and waspish action
Which she did use as she was writing of it,   10
It bears an angry tenour: pardon me;
I am but as a guiltless messenger.
   Rosalind. Patience herself would startle at this letter,
And play the swaggerer: bear this, bear all:
She says I am not fair; that I lack manners;   15
She calls me proud, and that she could not love me
Were man as rare as phœnix. 'Od's my will!
Her love is not the hare that I do hunt:
Why writes she so to me? Well, shepherd, well,
This is a letter of your own device.   20
   Silvius. No, I protest, I know not the contents:
Phebe did write it.
   Rosalind.   Come, come, you are a fool,
And turn'd into the extremity of love.
I saw her hand: she has a leathern hand,
A freestone-colour'd hand; I verily did think   25
That her old gloves were on, but 'twas her hands:
She has a housewife's hand; but that's no matter:
I say she never did invent this letter;
This is a man's invention, and his hand.
   Silvius. Sure, it is hers.   30
   Rosalind. Why, 'tis a boisterous and a cruel style,
A style for challengers; why, she defies me,
Like Turk to Christian: women's gentle brain

---

14 **play the swaggerer:** turn provocative.   **bear . . . all:** if
I endure this, I would endure anything.   20 **device:** devising, inventing.   23 **turn'd into:** brought into.   29 **hand:** handwriting.

Could not drop forth such giant-rude invention,
Such Ethiop words, blacker in their effect   85
Than in their countenance. Will you hear the letter?
  Silvius. So please you, for I never heard it yet;
Yet heard too much of Phebe's cruelty.
  Rosalind. She Phebes me. Mark how the tyrant writes.
[*Reads.*]

        Art thou god to shepherd turn'd,
        That a maiden's heart hath burn'd?   40

Can a woman rail thus?
  Silvius. Call you this railing?
  Rosalind. [*reads.*]

        Why, thy godhead laid apart,
        Warr'st thou with a woman's heart?   45

Did you ever hear such railing?

        Whiles the eye of man did woo me,
        That could do no vengeance to me.

Meaning me a beast.

        If the scorn of your bright eyne   50
        Have power to raise such love in mine,
        Alack! in me what strange effect
        Would they work in mild aspect.
        Whiles you chid me, I did love;
        How then might your prayers move!   55
        He that brings this love to thee
        Little knows this love in me;
        And by him seal up thy mind;
        Whether that thy youth and kind
        Will the faithful offer take   60
        Of me and all that I can make;
        Or else by him my love deny,
        And then I'll study how to die.

36 countenance: appearance (of the black ink).   **48 vengeance**: mischief.   **50 eyne**: eyes.   **53 in mild aspect**: if they looked favourably on me [*N*].   **58 seal up thy mind**: send your answer by him in a sealed letter.   **59 kind**: nature.

Silvius. Call you this chiding?

Celia. Alas, poor shepherd!   65

Rosalind. Do you pity him? no, he deserves no pity.
Wilt thou love such a woman? What, to make thee
an instrument and play false strains upon thee! not to
be endured! Well, go your way to her, for I see love
hath made thee a tame snake, and say this to her: that 70
if she love me, I charge her to love thee: if she will not,
I will never have her, unless thou entreat for her. If
you be a true lover, hence, and not a word, for here
comes more company.   [*Exit* SILVIUS.

Enter OLIVER.

Oliver. Good morrow, fair ones. Pray you, if you know,
Where in the purlieus of this forest stands   76
A sheepcote fenc'd about with olive-trees?

Celia. West of this place, down in the neighbour bottom:
The rank of osiers by the murmuring stream
Left on your right hand brings you to the place.   80
But at this hour the house doth keep itself;
There's none within.

Oliver. If that an eye may profit by a tongue,
Then should I know you by description;
Such garments, and such years: 'The boy is fair,   85
Of female favour, and bestows himself
Like a ripe sister: the woman low,
And browner than her brother.' Are not you
The owner of the house I did inquire for?

Celia. It is no boast, being ask'd, to say, we are.   90

Oliver. Orlando doth commend him to you both,

68 **instrument**: (i) tool and (ii) musical instrument.   **70 a
tame snake**: a poor creature [*N*].   **76 purlieus**: tracts of land on
the fringe of a forest.   **78 bottom**: dale, valley.   **79 rank**:
row.   **83 If . . . tongue**: if I can recognize you by what has been
told me.   **86–7 Of female favour . . . like a ripe sister**: female in
appearance and behaves like a mature (and so elder) sister [*N*].

And to that youth he calls his Rosalind
He sends this bloody napkin. Are you he?

   Rosalind. I am: what must we understand by this?

   Oliver. Some of my shame; if you will know of me   95
What man I am, and how, and why, and where
This handkercher was stain'd.

   Celia.   I pray you, tell it.

   Oliver. When last the young Orlando parted from you
He left a promise to return again
Within an hour; and, pacing through the forest,   100
Chewing the food of sweet and bitter fancy,
Lo, what befell! he threw his eye aside,
And mark what object did present itself:
Under an oak, whose boughs were moss'd with age,
And high top bald with dry antiquity,   105
A wretched ragged man, o'ergrown with hair,
Lay sleeping on his back: about his neck
A green and gilded snake had wreath'd itself,
Who with her head nimble in threats approach'd
The opening of his mouth; but suddenly,   110
Seeing Orlando, it unlink'd itself,
And with indented glides did slip away
Into a bush; under which bush's shade
A lioness, with udders all drawn dry,
Lay couching, head on ground, with catlike watch,   115
When that the sleeping man should stir; for 'tis
The royal disposition of that beast
To prey on nothing that doth seem as dead:
This seen, Orlando did approach the man,
And found it was his brother, his elder brother.   120

   Celia. O! I have heard him speak of that same brother;
And he did render him the most unnatural

---

   93 napkin: handkerchief.   **101 sweet and bitter fancy:**
alternately hopeful and despondent [*N*].   **112 indented:** zigzag.
122 render: describe.

That liv'd 'mongst men.

   Oliver.   And well he might so do,

For well I know he was unnatural.   **124**

   Rosalind. But, to Orlando: did he leave him there,

Food to the suck'd and hungry lioness?

   Oliver. Twice did he turn his back and purpos'd so:

But kindness, nobler ever than revenge,

And nature, stronger than his just occasion,

Made him give battle to the lioness,   **130**

Who quickly fell before him: in which hurtling

From miserable slumber I awak'd.

   Celia. Are you his brother?

   Rosalind.   Was it you he rescu'd?

   Celia. Was't you that did so oft contrive to kill him?

   Oliver. 'Twas I; but 'tis not I. I do not shame   **135**

To tell you what I was, since my conversion

So sweetly tastes, being the thing I am.

   Rosalind. But, for the bloody napkin?

   Oliver.   By and by.

When from the first to last, betwixt us two,

Tears our recountments had most kindly bath'd,   **140**

As how I came into that desert place:—

In brief, he led me to the gentle duke,

Who gave me fresh array and entertainment,

Committing me unto my brother's love;

Who led me instantly unto his cave,   **145**

There stripp'd himself; and here, upon his arm

The lioness had torn some flesh away,

Which all this while had bled; and now he fainted,

And cried, in fainting, upon Rosalind.

Brief, I recover'd him, bound up his wound;   **150**

---

  129 **just occasion:** the sound reason which gave a legitimate excuse, i.e. for leaving Oliver to his fate.   131 **hurtling:** tumult. 140 **recountments:** narratives.   141 **As:** such as.   150 **recover'd:** restored (transitive use of 'recover').

And, after some small space, being strong at heart,
He sent me hither, stranger as I am,
To tell this story, that you might excuse
His broken promise; and to give this napkin,
Dy'd in his blood, unto the shepherd youth   **155**
That he in sport doth call his Rosalind.

    Celia. [ROSALIND *swoons.*] Why, how now, Ganymede!
sweet Ganymede!

    Oliver. Many will swoon when they do look on blood.

    Celia. There is more in it. Cousin! Ganymede!

    Oliver. Look, he recovers.   **160**

    Rosalind. I would I were at home.

    Celia.   We'll lead you thither.
I pray you, will you take him by the arm?

    Oliver. Be of good cheer, youth. You a man! You lack
a man's heart.   **164**

    Rosalind. I do so, I confess it. Ah, sirrah! a body would
think this was well counterfeited. I pray you, tell your
brother how well I counterfeited. Heigh-ho!

    Oliver. This was not counterfeit: there is too great testi-
mony in your complexion that it was a passion of earnest.

    Rosalind. Counterfeit, I assure you.   **170**

    Oliver. Well then, take a good heart and counterfeit to
be a man.

    Rosalind. So I do; but, i' faith, I should have been a
woman by right.   **174**

    Celia. Come; you look paler and paler: pray you, draw
homewards. Good sir, go with us.

    Oliver. That will I, for I must bear answer back
How you excuse my brother, Rosalind.

    Rosalind. I shall devise something. But, I pray you, com-
mend my counterfeiting to him. Will you go?   [*Exeunt.*

---

       169 a passion of earnest: genuine grief.

ACT V

Scene I. THE FOREST OF ARDEN

Enter TOUCHSTONE *and* AUDREY.

Touchstone. We shall find a time, Audrey: patience, gentle Audrey.

Audrey. Faith, the priest was good enough, for all the old gentleman's saying.   4

Touchstone. A most wicked Sir Oliver, Audrey; a most vile Martext. But, Audrey, there is a youth here in the forest lays claim to you.

Audrey. Ay, I know who 'tis: he hath no interest in me in the world. Here comes the man you mean.   9

Enter WILLIAM.

Touchstone. It is meat and drink to me to see a clown. By my troth, we that have good wits have much to answer for: we shall be flouting; we cannot hold.

William. Good even, Audrey.

Audrey. God ye good even, William.

William. And good even to you, sir.   15

Touchstone. Good even, gentle friend. Cover thy head, cover thy head; nay, prithee, be covered. How old are you, friend?

William. Five-and-twenty, sir.

Touchstone. A ripe age. Is thy name William?   20

William. William, sir.

Touchstone. A fair name. Wast born i' the forest here?

William. Ay, sir, I thank God.

Touchstone. 'Thank God;' a good answer. Art rich?

---

12 **we shall be flouting: we** must jeer.   **hold: restrain** ourselves.   14 **God ye good even:** (one of several abbreviated forms of) God give you good even.

William. Faith, sir, so so.   25

Touchstone. 'So so,' is good, very good, very excellent good: and yet it is not; it is but so so. Art thou wise?

William. Ay, sir, I have a pretty wit.

Touchstone. Why, thou sayest well. I do now remember a saying, 'The fool doth think he is wise, but   30 the wise man knows himself to be a fool.' The heathen philosopher, when he had a desire to eat a grape, would open his lips when he put it into his mouth; meaning thereby that grapes were made to eat and lips to open. You do love this maid?   35

William. I do, sir.

Touchstone. Give me your hand. Art thou learned?

William. No, sir.

Touchstone. Then learn this of me: to have, is to have; for it is a figure in rhetoric, that drink, being   40 poured out of a cup into a glass, by filling the one doth empty the other; for all your writers do consent that *ipse* is he: now, you are not *ipse*, for I am he.

William. Which he, sir?

Touchstone. He, sir, that must marry this woman.   45 Therefore, you clown, abandon,—which is in the vulgar, leave,—the society,—which in the boorish is, company,—of this female,—which in the common is, woman; which together is, abandon the society of this female, or, clown, thou perishest; or, to thy better   50 understanding, diest; or, to wit, I kill thee, make thee away, translate thy life into death, thy liberty into bondage. I will deal in poison with thee, or in bastinado, or in steel; I will bandy with thee in faction; I will o'errun thee with policy; I will kill thee a hundred   55 and fifty ways: therefore tremble, and depart.

51 **to wit:** that is to say.   53 **bastinado:** severe beating with a cudgel.   54 **bandy with thee:** beat thee to and fro. **faction:** (party) strife.   55 **policy:** schemes and stratagems.

Audrey. Do, good William.

William. God rest you merry, sir.   [*Exit.*

Enter CORIN.

Corin. Our master and mistress seek you: come, away, away!   60

Touchstone. Trip, Audrey! trip, Audrey! I attend, I attend.   [*Exeunt.*

Scene II. ANOTHER PART OF THE FOREST

Enter ORLANDO *and* OLIVER.

Orlando. Is't possible that on so little acquaintance you should like her? that, but seeing, you should love her? and, loving, woo? and, wooing, she should grant? and will you persever to enjoy her?

Oliver. Neither call the giddiness of it in question, 5 the poverty of her, the small acquaintance, my sudden wooing, nor her sudden consenting; but say with me, I love Aliena; say with her, that she loves me; consent with both, that we may enjoy each other: it shall be to your good; for my father's house and all the revenue 10 that was old Sir Rowland's will I estate upon you, and here live and die a shepherd.

Orlando. You have my consent. Let your wedding be to-morrow: thither will I invite the duke and all's con-tented followers. Go you and prepare Aliena; for, look you, here comes my Rosalind.   16

Enter ROSALIND.

Rosalind. God save you, brother.

Oliver. And you, fair sister.   [*Exit.*

Rosalind. O! my dear Orlando, how it grieves me to see thee wear thy heart in a scarf.   20

---

4 persever: (accented persever) go on.   **5 giddiness:** haste,
rashness.   **11 estate:** settle.

Orlando. It is my arm.

Rosalind. I thought thy heart had been wounded with the claws of a lion.

Orlando. Wounded it is, but with the eyes of a lady.   24

Rosalind. Did your brother tell you how I counterfeited to swound when he showed me your handkercher?

Orlando. Ay, and greater wonders than that.

Rosalind. O! I know where you are. Nay, 'tis true: there was never anything so sudden but the fight of two rams, and Cæsar's thrasonical brag of 'I came, saw, and   30 overcame:' for your brother and my sister no sooner met, but they looked; no sooner looked but they loved; no sooner loved but they sighed; no sooner sighed but they asked one another the reason; no sooner knew the reason but they sought the remedy: and in these degrees   35 have they made a pair of stairs to marriage which they will climb incontinent, or else be incontinent before marriage. They are in the very wrath of love, and they will together: clubs cannot part them.

Orlando. They shall be married to-morrow, and I will   40 bid the duke to the nuptial. But, O! how bitter a thing it is to look into happiness through another man's eyes. By so much the more shall I to-morrow be at the height of heart-heaviness, by how much I shall think my brother happy in having what he wishes for.   45

Rosalind. Why then, to-morrow I cannot serve your turn for Rosalind?

Orlando. I can live no longer by thinking.

Rosalind. I will weary you then no longer with idle talking. Know of me then,—for now I speak to some   50 purpose,—that I know you are a gentleman of good

---

28 **I know where you are:** I know what you are at, to what you refer.   30 **thrasonical:** boastful [N].   35 **degrees:** stages (a pun with 'stairs', l. 36).   37 **incontinent:** forthwith. **incontinent:** unchaste.   38 **wrath:** passion.

conceit. I speak not this that you should bear a good
opinion of my knowledge, insomuch I say I know you
are; neither do I labour for a greater esteem than may in
some little measure draw a belief from you, to do your- 55
self good, and not to grace me. Believe then, if you
please, that I can do strange things. I have, since I was
three years old, conversed with a magician, most profound in his art and yet not damnable. If you do love
Rosalind so near the heart as your gesture cries it out, 60
when your brother marries Aliena, shall you marry her.
I know into what straits of fortune she is driven; and
it is not impossible to me, if it appear not inconvenient
to you, to set her before your eyes to-morrow, human
as she is, and without any danger. 65

Orlando. Speakest thou in sober meanings?

Rosalind. By my life, I do; which I tender dearly,
though I say I am a magician. Therefore, put you in
your best array; bid your friends; for if you will be married
to-morrow, you shall; and to Rosalind, if you will. Look,
here comes a lover of mine, and a lover of hers. 71

Enter SILVIUS *and* PHEBE.

Phebe. Youth, you have done me much ungentleness,
To show the letter that I writ to you.

Rosalind. I care not if I have: it is my study
To seem despiteful and ungentle to you. 75
You are there follow'd by a faithful shepherd;
Look upon him, love him; he worships you.

Phebe. Good shepherd, tell this youth what 'tis to love.

Silvius. It is to be all made of sighs and tears;
And so am I for Phebe. 80

Phebe. And I for Ganymede.

---

52 **conceit:** intelligence.   53 **insomuch:** inasmuch as.   60
gesture: bearing.   65 **danger:** dangerous magic.   67 **tender
dearly:** hold dear.   74 **study:** deliberate aim.

Orlando. And I for Rosalind.

Rosalind. And I for no woman.

Silvius. It is to be all made of faith and service;
And so am I for Phebe.   85

Phebe. And I for Ganymede.

Orlando. And I for Rosalind.

Rosalind. And I for no woman.

Silvius. It is to be all made of fantasy,
All made of passion, and all made of wishes;   90
All adoration, duty, and observance;
All humbleness, all patience, and impatience;
All purity, all trial, all obeisance;
And so am I for Phebe.

Phebe. And so am I for Ganymede.   95

Orlando. And so am I for Rosalind.

Rosalind. And so am I for no woman.

Phebe. [*To* ROSALIND.] If this be so, why blame you me
to love you?

Silvius. [*To* PHEBE.] If this be so, why blame you me
to love you?   101

Orlando. If this be so, why blame you me to love you?

Rosalind. Who do you speak to, 'Why blame you me
to love you?'

Orlando. To her that is not here, nor doth not hear.   105

Rosalind. Pray you, no more of this: 'tis like the howling of Irish wolves against the moon. [*To* SILVIUS.] I
will help you, if I can: [*To* PHEBE.] I would love you,
if I could. To-morrow meet me all together. [*To*
PHEBE.] I will marry you, if ever I marry woman, and 110
I'll be married to-morrow: [*To* ORLANDO.] I will
satisfy you, if ever I satisfied man, and you shall be
married to-morrow: [*To* SILVIUS.] I will content you, if
what pleases you contents you, and you shall be

---

91 **observance**: respect [*N*].   93 **trial**: willingness to suffer.
104 **to love**: for loving.

married to-morrow. [*To* ORLANDO. As you love 115
Rosalind, meet: [*To* SILVIUS.] As you love Phebe,
meet: and as I love no woman, I'll meet. So, fare you
well: I have left you commands.

Silvius. I'll not fail, if I live.

Phebe. Nor I.   120

Orlando. Nor I.   [*Exeunt.*

Scene III. ANOTHER PART OF THE FOREST

Enter TOUCHSTONE *and* AUDREY.

Touchstone. To-morrow is the joyful day, Audrey; to-
morrow will we be married.

Audrey. I do desire it with all my heart, and I hope it
is no dishonest desire to desire to be a woman of the
world. Here come two of the banished duke's pages.   5

Enter two Pages.

First Page. Well met, honest gentleman.

Touchstone. By my troth, well met. Come, sit, sit, and
a song.

Second Page. We are for you: sit i' the middle.   9

First Page. Shall we clap into 't roundly, without hawking or spitting, or saying we are hoarse, which are the only
prologues to a bad voice?

Second Page. I' faith, i' faith; and both in a tune, like
two gipsies on a horse.

---

4 **dishonest:** immodest. 4–5 **a woman of the world:** a married
woman [*N*].   10 **clap into't roundly:** begin it briskly and without
hesitation.   **hawking:** clearing the throat.   11 **the only:**
only the.   13 **both in a tune:** both in unison (like two gipsies
on a horse).

SONG.

It was a lover and his lass,   15
    With a hey, and a ho, and a hey nonino,
That o'er the green corn-field did pass,
    In the spring time, the only pretty ring time,
When birds do sing, hey ding a ding, ding;
Sweet lovers love the spring.   20

Between the acres of the rye,
    With a hey, and a ho, and a hey nonino,
These pretty country folks would lie,
    In the spring time, &c.

This carol they began that hour,   25
    With a hey, and a ho, and a hey nonino,
How that a life was but a flower
    In the spring time, &c.

And therefore take the present time,
    With a hey, and a ho, and a hey nonino;   30
For love is crowned with the prime
    In the spring time, &c.

Touchstone. Truly, young gentlemen, though there was no great matter in the ditty, yet the note was very untuneable.   35

First Page. You are deceived, sir: we kept time; we lost not our time.

Touchstone. By my troth, yes; I count it but time lost to hear such a foolish song. God be wi' you; and God mend your voices! Come, Audrey.   [*Exeunt.*

Scene IV. ANOTHER PART OF THE FOREST

Enter DUKE *Senior*, AMIENS, JAQUES, ORLANDO, OLIVER, *and* CELIA.

Duke Senior. Dost thou believe, Orlando, that the boy Can do all this that he hath promised?

---

18 **the only pretty ring time:** the time most suitable for marriage.   25 **carol:** song for a festival (originally a ring-dance with a song).   31 **prime:** (i) spring-time and (ii) the highest perfection.

Orlando. I sometimes do believe, and sometimes do not;
As those that fear they hope, and know they fear.

      Enter ROSALIND, SILVIUS, *and* PHEBE.

Rosalind. Patience once more, whiles our compact is
  urg'd.   5
[*To the* DUKE.] You say, if I bring in your Rosalind,
You will bestow her on Orlando here?
  Duke Senior. That would I, had I kingdoms to give with
  her.
  Rosalind. [*To* ORLANDO.] And you say, you will have
  her when I bring her?
  Orlando. That would I, were I of all kingdoms king. 10
  Rosalind [*To* PHEBE.] You say, you'll marry me, if I be
  willing?
  Phebe. That will I, should I die the hour after.
  Rosalind. But if you do refuse to marry me,
You'll give yourself to this most faithful shepherd?
  Phebe. So is the bargain.   15
  Rosalind. [*To* SILVIUS.] You say, that you'll have Phebe,
  if she will?
  Silvius. Though to have her and death were both one
  thing.
  Rosalind. I have promis'd to make all this matter even.
Keep you your word, O duke, to give your daughter;
You yours, Orlando, to receive his daughter;   20
Keep you your word, Phebe, that you'll marry me,
Or else, refusing me, to wed this shepherd;
Keep your word, Silvius, that you'll marry her,
If she refuse me: and from hence I go,
To make these doubts all even.   25
            [*Exeunt* ROSALIND *and* CELIA.
  Duke Senior. I do remember in this shepherd boy
Some lively touches of my daughter's favour.

    18 even: smooth, right.   **27 favour:** appearance.

Orlando. My lord, the first time that I ever saw him,
Methought he was a brother to your daughter;
But, my good lord, this boy is forest-born,   30
And hath been tutor'd in the rudiments
Of many desperate studies by his uncle,
Whom he reports to be a great magician,
Obscured in the circle of this forest.

Enter TOUCHSTONE *and* AUDREY.

Jaques. There is, sure, another flood toward, and these
couples are coming to the ark. Here comes a pair of very
strange beasts, which in all tongues are called fools.   37

Touchstone. Salutation and greeting to you all!

Jaques. Good my lord, bid him welcome. This is the
motley-minded gentleman that I have so often met in the
forest: he hath been a courtier, he swears.   41

Touchstone. If any man doubt that, let him put me to
my purgation. I have trod a measure; I have flattered a
lady; I have been politic with my friend, smooth with
mine enemy; I have undone three tailors; I have had
four quarrels, and like to have fought one.   46

Jaques. And how was that ta'en up?

Touchstone. Faith, we met, and found the quarrel was
upon the seventh cause.

Jaques. How seventh cause? Good my lord, like this
fellow.   51

Duke Senior. I like him very well.

Touchstone. God 'ild you, sir; I desire you of the like.
I press in here, sir, amongst the rest of the country
copulatives, to swear, and to forswear, according as   55

---

35 toward: at hand.   **43 purgation:** trial.   **trod a measure:**
danced a slow and stately dance [*N*].   **44 politic:** underhand.
45 undone: ruined.   **47 ta'en up:** made up, arranged.   **53 I
desire you of the like:** I wish you to remain in the same mood.
55 copulatives: those wishing to marry.

marriage binds and blood breaks. A poor virgin, sir, an ill-favoured thing, sir, but mine own: a poor humour of mine, sir, to take that that no man else will. Rich honesty dwells like a miser, sir, in a poor house, as your pearl in your foul oyster.   60

Duke S. By my faith, he is very swift and sententious.

Touchstone. According to the fool's bolt, sir, and such dulcet diseases.

Jaques. But, for the seventh cause; how did you find the quarrel on the seventh cause?   65

Touchstone. Upon a lie seven times removed:—bear your body more seeming, Audrey:—as thus, sir. I did dislike the cut of a certain courtier's beard: he sent me word, if I said his beard was not cut well, he was in the mind it was: this is called 'the retort courteous.' If I   70 sent him word again, it was not well cut, he would send me word, he cut it to please himself: this is called the 'quip modest.' If again, it was not well cut, he disabled my judgment: this is called the 'reply churlish.' If again, it was not well cut, he would answer, I spake   75 not true: this is called the 'reproof valiant;' if again, it was not well cut, he would say, I lie: this is called the 'countercheck quarrelsome:' and so to the 'lie circumstantial,' and the 'lie direct.'   79

Jaques. And how oft did you say his beard was not well cut?

Touchstone. I durst go no further than the 'lie circumstantial,' nor he durst not give me the 'lie direct;' and so we measured swords and parted.

Jaques. Can you nominate in order now the degrees of the lie?   85

---

56 blood breaks: passion breaks the marriage vow.   63
dulcet: sweet [*N*].   **67 seeming:** becomingly.   **68 dislike:** express my dislike of.   **73 quip:** sarcastic retort.   **disabled:** disallowed the validity of.   **78 lie circumstantial:** i.e. only a lie in certain circumstances.

Touchstone. O sir, we quarrel in print; by the book, as
you have books for good manners: I will name you the
degrees. The first, the 'retort courteous;' the second
the 'quip modest;' the third, the 'reply churlish;' the
fourth, the 'reproof valiant;' the fifth, the 'counter- 90
check quarrelsome;' the sixth, the 'lie with circumstance;' the seventh, the 'lie direct.' All these you
may avoid but the lie direct; and you may avoid that
too, with an 'if.' I knew when seven justices could not
take up a quarrel; but when the parties were met 95
themselves, one of them thought but of an 'if,' as 'If
you said so, then I said so;' and they shook hands and
swore brothers. Your 'if' is the only peace-maker;
much virtue in 'if.'

Jaques. Is not this a rare fellow, my lord? he's as good
at any thing, and yet a fool. 101

Duke Senior. He uses his folly like a stalking-horse, and
under the presentation of that he shoots his wit.

Enter HYMEN, *leading* ROSALIND *in woman's clothes, and* CELIA.
Still Music.

Hymen. Then is there mirth in heaven,
When earthly things made even 105
Atone together.
Good duke, receive thy daughter;
Hymen from heaven brought her;
Yea, brought her hither,
That thou mightst join her hand with his, 110
Whose heart within his bosom is.

Rosalind. [*To* DUKE SENIOR.] To you I give myself, for
I am yours.

[*To* ORLANDO.] To you I give myself, for I am yours.

86 **by the book:** according to the book [*N*].   102 **stalking-
horse:** a horse under cover of which a sportsman approaches the
game, hence a pretext.   103 **presentation:** show, appearance.
106 **atone:** are reconciled.   111 **Whose:** the antecedent is 'her' [*N*].

Duke Senior.   If there be truth in sight, you are my
    daughter.   114
Orlando. If there be truth in sight, you are my Rosalind.
Phebe. If sight and shape be true,
Why then, my love adieu!
    Rosalind. [*To* DUKE SENIOR] I'll have no father, if you
    be not he.]
[*To* ORLANDO.] I'll have no husband, if you be not he:
[*To* PHEBE.] Nor ne'er wed woman, if you be not she. 120
    Hymen. Peace, ho! I bar confusion:
        'Tis I must make conclusion
            Of these most strange events:
        Here's eight that must take hands
        To join in Hymen's bands,   125
            If truth holds true contents.
    [*To* ORLANDO *and* ROSALIND.] You and you no
        cross shall part:
    [*To* OLIVER *and* CELIA.] You and you are heart
        in heart:
    [*To* PHEBE.] You to his love must accord,
    Or have a woman to your lord: 130
    [*To* TOUCHSTONE *and* AUDREY.] You and you are
        sure together,
    As the winter to foul weather.
    Whiles a wedlock hymn we sing,
    Feed yourselves with questioning,
    That reason wonder may diminish,   135
    How thus we met, and these things finish.

SONG.

    Wedding is great Juno's crown:
        O blessed bond of board and bed!
    'Tis Hymen peoples every town;
        High wedlock then be honoured.   140

121 **bar:** prohibit.   126 **hold true contents:** is really itself.
140 **High:** highly (i.e. adverb not adjective).

Honour, high honour, and renown,
To Hymen, god of every town!

Duke Senior. O my dear niece! welcome thou art to me:
Even daughter, welcome in no less degree.
Phebe. [*To* SILVIUS.] I will not eat my word, now thou
    art mine;   145
Thy faith my fancy to thee doth combine.

Enter JAQUES DE BOYS.

Jaques de Boys. Let me have audience for a word or two:
I am the second son of old Sir Rowland,
That bring these tidings to this fair assembly.
Duke Frederick, hearing how that every day   150
Men of great worth resorted to this forest,
Address'd a mighty power, which were on foot
In his own conduct, purposely to take
His brother here and put him to the sword:
And to the skirts of this wild wood he came,   155
Where, meeting with an old religious man,
After some question with him, was converted
Both from his enterprise and from the world;
His crown bequeathing to his banish'd brother,
And all their lands restor'd to them again   160
That were with him exil'd. This to be true,
I do engage my life.
    Duke Senior.   Welcome, young man;
Thou offer'st fairly to thy brothers' wedding:
To one, his lands withheld; and to the other
A land itself at large, a potent dukedom.   165

---

146 combine: bind.   152 Address'd: made ready.   power:
army.   153 In his own conduct: under his own leadership.
157 question: talk.   163 offer'st fairly: makest a handsome
offering.   164 To one . . . and to the other: (i) to Oliver and
(ii) to Orlando [N].   165 at large: in absolute possession.

First, in this forest, let us do those ends
That here were well begun and well begot;
And after, every of this happy number
That have endur'd shrewd days and nights with us,
Shall share the good of our returned fortune,   170
According to the measure of their states.
Meantime, forget this new-fall'n dignity,
And fall into our rustic revelry.
Play, music! and you, brides and bridegrooms all,
With measure heap'd in joy, to the measures fall.   175

   Jaques. Sir, by your patience. If I heard you rightly,
The duke hath put on a religious life,
And thrown into neglect the pompous court?

   Jaques de Boys. He hath.

   Jaques. To him will I: out of these convertites   180
There is much matter to be heard and learn'd.
[*To* DUKE SENIOR.] You to your former honour I bequeath;
Your patience and your virtue well deserves it:
[*To* ORLANDO.] You to a love that your true faith doth
    merit: 184
[*To* OLIVER.] You to your land, and love, and great allies:
[*To* SILVIUS.] You to a long and well-deserved bed:
[*To* TOUCHSTONE.] And you to wrangling; for thy loving
    voyage
Is but for two months victual'd. So, to your pleasures:
I am for other than for dancing measures.

   Duke Senior. Stay, Jaques, stay.   190

   Jaques. To see no pastime, I: what you would have
I'll stay to know at your abandon'd cave.   [*Exit.*

   Duke Senior. Proceed, proceed: we will begin these rites,
As we do trust they'll end, in true delights.
                        [*A dance. Exeunt.*

---

166 do those ends: complete those purposes. **168 every:** every one.
169 shrewd: bitter, grievous. **171 states:** estates. **175 measures:**
formal dances. **180 convertites:** converts. **186 bed:** i.e. wife.

EPILOGUE

SPOKEN BY ROSALIND.

It is not the fashion to see the lady the epilogue; but it is no 195
more unhandsome than to see the lord the prologue. If it be
true that good wine needs no bush, 'tis true that a good play
needs no epilogue; yet to good wine they do use good bushes,
and good plays prove the better by the help of good epilogues.
What a case am I in then, that am neither a good epilogue, 200
nor cannot insinuate with you in the behalf of a good play!
I am not furnished like a beggar, therefore to beg will not
become me: my way is, to conjure you; and I'll begin with
the women. I charge you, O women! for the love you bear
to men, to like as much of this play as please you: and I 205
charge you, O men! for the love you bear to women,—as I
perceive by your simpering none of you hate them,—that
between you and the women, the play may please. If I
were a woman I would kiss as many of you as had beards
that pleased me, complexions that liked me, and breaths 210
that I defied not; and, I am sure, as many as have good
beards, or good faces, or sweet breaths, will, for my kind
offer, when I make curtsy, bid me farewell.   [*Exeunt.*

---

201 **insinuate with you:** win your favour.   203 **conjure
you:** appeal to you.   210 **liked:** pleased.   211 **defied:** hated,
rejected.

NOTES

F. = First Folio of 1623.

Lodge = Lodge's novel, *Rosalynde*.

O.E.D. = *Oxford English Dictionary*.

References to other plays are made to the one volume Oxford Shakespeare.

Textual notes and a few other more advanced notes are enclosed within brackets, thus [ ].

ACT I. SCENE I

In this opening scene Shakespeare very skilfully conveys the two situations round which the main action of the play revolves. Their theme is the same, the unnatural relations between two brothers: Orlando and Oliver, the banished Duke and the usurper Frederick. But already in this first scene, with its sympathetic drawing of the misused Orlando and the graceful hint of the love uniting Rosalind and Celia, it is clear that the romantic variations and developments will become more important than the theme itself.

1–4. As I remember . . . breed me well. Orlando and Adam are found in the middle of a discussion of the dead Sir Rowland's will and his eldest son's carrying out of its terms. Orlando says: 'In this way I was left a paltry thousand crowns, but, as you, Adam, have just reminded me, my father charged my brother to provide suitably for my upbringing if he would earn his dying blessing.'

> [Of several attempts to correct this grammatically faulty sentence the following may be noted: (i) it was upon this fashion: a' (= he) bequeathed me by will; (ii) a poor thousand crowns; (iii) a' charged my brother. It would be an endless and obviously mistaken task to correct Shakespeare's syntax and complete his anacoloutha in every detail, especially where the speaker, as here, is in the full tide of intimate, informal conversation. In such talk, the meaning of this sentence is perfectly clear; and Shakespeare may well have written it as it stands in the text. The transposed 'poor a' for 'a poor' gives emphasis.]

5. Jaques. This is the only mention of the second son by name, which Shakespeare takes from Lodge. When he appears in person (v. iv. 147) the Folio calls him merely 'Second Brother', for long before that stage is reached the name Jaques is inalienably associated with the banished Duke's melancholy follower, and another Jaques would cause confusion. Shakespeare seems to have overlooked the use of the name here. For the pronunciation, see note to II. i. 26.

5. **school:** used for both school and University: Hamlet was 'at school in Wittenberg' (*Hamlet*, I. ii. 113).

36. **keep your hogs, and eat husks:** a reference to the story of the prodigal son (Luke xv. 16), which explains the meaning of 'prodigal portion' = the portion of a prodigal son.

41. **him:** he whom, with the first pronoun attracted into the case of the (omitted) second.

50. **What, boy!** A blow from Oliver, accompanying these words, explains Orlando's next speech. He apparently resists, successfully (cf. l. 58); hence the taunt (ll. 51–2) to the elder brother who is less experienced than he 'in this', i.e. in fighting. Orlando's prowess suggests the wrestling match to Oliver (l. 86) as a way of revenge.

55. **de Boys.** Shakespeare may have taken the name of de Boys from a medieval family which held the manor of Weston-in-Arden.

74. **will.** By 'will' Shakespeare implies both 'wish' and 'what was left Orlando by his father's will'. Note here, again in l. 82, and frequently throughout, Shakespeare's play on the double meaning of words.

110. **forest of Arden.** In Lodge's *Rosalynde* this is the ancient forest of Ardennes in Flanders. To Shakespeare and his audience it became the forest of Arden in Warwickshire, with which *As You Like It* is for ever identified in English minds, although in fact the name occurs only three times in the play: here, I. iii. 104, and II. iv. 12. Some critics, wrote Knight, 'maintain that its geographical position (i.e. that of 'Arden') ought to have been known by Shakespeare, and that he is consequently most vehemently to be reprehended for imagining that a palm-tree could flourish, and a lioness be starving, in French Flanders. We most heartily wish that the critics would allow poetry to have its own geography,'—and, one may add, its own fauna and flora.

111. **a many.** In Elizabethan English 'a' is often inserted before numeral adjectives, as here.

112. **the old Robin Hood of England.** Already by the fourteenth century Robin Hood was the hero of popular ballads, and many rhyming stories of his various exploits were current in Shakespeare's time. It is sad to have to admit that this very English outlaw, with Maid Marian and his band of merry men, probably never existed in Sherwood Forest or anywhere else, except in the popular imagination.

114. **golden world.** The 'golden age' was a legendary period in human history, in a remote past, when mankind was entirely free, innocent, and happy—and apparently had no work to do, for the earth yielded its riches in abundance. See *The Tempest*, II. i. 150–75.

133. **underhand.** This does not mean deceptive, but merely 'not obvious', since, Oliver implies, openly expressed advice would have been useless with such a fire-eater as, in order to rouse Charles, he represents Orlando to be.

134. **it:** often used in Elizabethan English for he or she, generally with familiar or even contemptuous meaning.

ACT I. SCENE II

In this scene we meet Rosalind and Celia, and see their love for one another, the loyalty and sympathetic charm of Celia, the high-spirited courage of the witty Rosalind. We are introduced, too, to Touchstone, the licensed 'fool' who is so much wiser than many of the so-called wise men, and thus becomes the mouthpiece of some of Shakespeare's shrewdest comment on life in the play. The wrestling-match takes place, and occasions the meeting and sudden, passionate falling in love of Rosalind and Orlando. Through all the glancing talk the action moves only less swiftly than the revelation of every essential character save those whom we shall meet later in Arden.

1. **sweet my coz.** The possessive, when unemphatic, is often so transposed in Shakespeare.

[F. reads: 'would you yet were merrier'.]

thou lovest me not. After her simple appeal to Rosalind to cheer up Celia has recourse to rather forced reasoning which her cousin at once sees through, though she responds and tries to be gay. Celia is seeking to talk her out of her sorrow, by inveigling her into the kind of witty argument in which, as will be seen later, Rosalind delighted.

29–30. **the good housewife Fortune from her wheel.** The image of Fortune as a blind female figure guiding an ever-turning wheel, thus bringing bad luck after good, was a long-established favourite (e.g. in Chaucer). The inconstancy of her gifts, and therefore, presumably, of Fortune herself, is here jestingly conveyed in the slightly contemptuous 'house-wife', often pronounced 'hussif' (hence 'hussy').

38–49. Fortune's office ... Nature's. The argument is that money, success, happiness, and the like, are Fortune's gifts: beauty, virtue, brains, are Nature's. In reply to Celia (ll. 35–7) Rosalind says (ll. 38–40): Now you are mixing up Fortune's business (i.e. money and human happiness) with Nature's (i.e. beauty and virtue). Celia retorts (l. 41) that a woman endowed with beauty (Nature) may go wrong by accident (Fortune). Shakespeare, and the Elizabethans generally, delighted in this kind of argument, involving a rapid play on words. But fashions in wit change, and some modern readers and audiences find such passages tedious.

49. [perceiving. F. has 'perceiveth'. We must either insert 'and' before 'hath sent', or adopt 'perceiving' from F. 2.]

51. whetstone. This is sometimes taken as a pun on Touchstone's name. But that is not actually spoken until ɪɪ. iv. 16, so that Celia's pun, if it be one, would be incomprehensible to the audience, who as yet know him only as the 'fool' (l. 44); and that would be bad dramatic business on Shakespeare's part. He may, of course, merely have forgotten that he has not already named him.

52–3. wit! whither wander you?: a jest at the wandering wits of the fool. For the expression, see also ɪv. i. 146.

55. messenger. Celia thinks Touchstone should have addressed her more politely, and her curt reply plays on a double meaning: 'messenger' is both messenger and police officer.

76–8. [old Frederick. In F. the speech headings of the two Dukes are simply 'Duke' and 'Duke Senior'. Nowhere in the play does the name of the elder Duke occur; the younger, the usurper, is directly mentioned as 'Duke Frederick' in v. iv. 150, and he is clearly the 'Frederick' referred to by Orlando in ɪ. ii. 219. But there is a difficulty in the present passage, for F. makes Rosalind, not Celia, reply: 'My father's love ...' in l. 77. It has been argued that this is right, because 'old' must refer to Duke Senior, and because even a licensed fool would hardly dare to refer to an autocratic usurper as 'old Frederick', especially to his own daughter. But 'old' need not emphasize his age, and Touchstone was a greatly privileged person. It is of course possible that Shakespeare carelessly wrote 'Frederick' and forgot to alter it; but, bearing all this in mind, the simplest way of dealing with his mistake (or that of the editors of F.) seems to be to adopt Theobald's emendation and give the speech (ll. 77–9) to Celia.]

77. [Many editors put a stop after 'him', and interpret 'enough!' as a check to Touchstone's chatter. The punctuation of F., as in the text, gives the sentence a good Shakespearian ring and meaning.]

82–3 since ... silenced. Celia's words probably refer to some recent official inhibition of books or plays; perhaps to the Order of 1 June 1599, suppressing the pamphlets written by Thomas Nashe and the scholar Gabriel Harvey in the course of a literary quarrel that made considerable stir.

92. [**sport.** Celia may be pretending to misunderstand Le Beau's affected pronunciation by asking the colour of the 'spot'. But 'colour' was used generally to mean appearance or quality: cf. 'a fellow of the self-same colour' in *Lear*, II. ii. 145.]

97. laid on with a trowel. The three are ridiculing Le Beau's affectations. Touchstone's 'the Destinies decree' apparently imitates his habit of pompous speech, and Celia praises his cleverness in even going beyond Le Beau in pompousness. (The expression 'lay on with a trowel' was used to mean 'to express a thing coarsely or bluntly' (*O.E.D.*); now, generally, for excessive flattery.) Touchstone replies that he must try to maintain his 'rank' as a clever fool, and Rosalind keeps the ball of wit rolling with a pun on 'rank' applied to a strong smell. Le Beau, as his next remark shows, is utterly bamboozled by these verbal fireworks.

108. There comes . . . sons. This is like the opening of a fairy-tale, as Celia promptly says.

110–11. growth and presence. Rosalind ridicules this pompous phrase by a pun on 'presence' and 'presents', meaning the opening words or statements of legal documents and proclamations or, as she calls them, 'bills'.

129. [**see.** Dr. Johnson suggested 'feel' for 'see', and this has often been adopted. But he himself wondered 'if any change were necessary . . . "see" is the colloquial term for perception or experiment'.]

129–30. broken music: probably part-music, i.e. played by various instruments or sung by various voices.

151. [**the princess calls.** The inconsistency between 'the princess calls' and Orlando's 'I attend them' has given rise to various conjectures; in the main that 'them' (l. 153) should be changed to 'her', or that the F. 'princesse' is a concealed plural (Shakespeare's ear rejecting the three sibilants of 'princesses', which never occurs in his plays), and that the compositor, reading it as a singular, added an 's' to 'cal'. But it may be argued that Orlando sees Rosalind and Celia standing together, guesses who they are (though not which is which, see l. 254), and replies, quite naturally, 'I attend them'. Perhaps it is forcing a point to maintain, like Professor Dover Wilson, that Orlando's 'them' is a sign of his allegiance to the banished Duke and his daughter in coupling her with her temporarily more royal cousin.]

170. wherein. The 'antecedent' of this very loosely used 'wherein' is the behaviour which brings down on Orlando the punishment of their hard thoughts, i.e. the denying them anything.

192. [Many editors, following Theobald, insert 'And' or 'An' (= If) before 'You mean to mock', some arguing that the compositor misread his manuscript: 'Orl. And' as 'Orland'. The meaning is clear without this: 'So you mean to mock me after our first fall', says Orlando. 'You should not have mocked me before it' (for that is the kind of presumption that brings swift revenge). Pride, in fact, goeth before a fall.]

194. Hercules be thy speed. Rosalind wishes that Hercules, the god of strength, and so of wrestlers, will lend his aid.

196. [The F. Stage Directions 'Wrastle' and, l. 199, 'Shout' suggest that they were printed from a prompt-copy used in the theatre.]

217. more proud: presumably than of being the son of 'another father' approved by the Duke.

218. calling. The word in this sense is rare, and without parallel elsewhere in Shakespeare.

231. out of suits with fortune. The metaphor, in this famous phrase, is probably taken from cards: one who cannot play Fortune's suit. It seems forced to see in it a reference to a dismissed servant who thus loses the suit or livery of the mistress, Fortune.

233. Shall we go, coz? Rosalind, suddenly realizing that this is love at first sight, and the consequent threat to her self-possession, instinctively tries to break off talk and call Celia away with her. It is a very natural touch when Celia, a little later (l. 240) has to urge her to go.

236. quintain. 'The quintain, originally, was no more than the trunk of a tree or post set up for the practice of the tyros in chivalry. Afterwards a staff or spear was fixed in the earth, and a shield being hung upon it, was the mark to strike at; the dexterity of the performer consisted in smiting the shield in such a manner as to break the ligatures and bear it to the ground.' (Strutt: *Sports and Pastimes*, i. 2, 239.)

250. misconsters: the old form and pronunciation of 'misconstrues': Shakespeare uses both forms.

251. humorous. The Elizabethan meaning of this word may be best seen in a passage in Ben Jonson's *Every Man Out of His Humour: Induction*, l. 102:

> 'As when some one peculiar quality
> Doth so possess a man, that it doth draw
> All his affects, his spirits, and his powers,
> In their confluctions, all to run one way,
> This may be truly said to be a humour.'

In this sense, obduracy is the Duke's 'humour'.

257. [**smaller.** F. has 'taller'. But in ɪv. iii. 87 Oliver describes Celia (Aliena) thus:

> 'the woman low,
> And browner than her brother';

and in ɪ. iii. 112 Rosalind describes herself as 'more than common
tall'. 'Taller' here may therefore be a slip, or Shakespeare—perhaps
in revising the play—may have changed his mind about Rosalind's
height, as he did about Hamlet's age, and forgotten to correct this.]

ACT I. Scene III

The Duke's anger against Rosalind breaks out, and he orders her
from his Court, in spite of the pleading of Celia, who at once decides
to accompany her cousin. The two plan to set out for Arden,
Rosalind disguised as a boy, and taking Touchstone to cheer them in
their wanderings. With these three (and Orlando) dismissed, the
Court is emptied of the only likeable people we have met in it.

11. **child's father:** i.e. the man I would like to marry, Orlando.
Rosalind is frankly confessing her immediate love for him.

14. **holiday foolery.** Rosalind's feeling for Orlando, Celia argues,
is but a passing hurt which she has picked up in a moment's
trifling. If two princesses deviate from their condition in talking
freely with an unknown young man ('walk not in the trodden
paths') they must expect to incur some annoyance thereby.

18. **Hem them away.** Note the puns: first, on the two meanings
of 'burr': (a) a prickly seed-case and (b) a thickness of utterance,
a choking sensation in the throat; and, l. 20, on 'hem' and 'him'.

24–5. **you will try . . . fall.** Celia keeps up the wrestling metaphor:
'You have lost the first round, but will try another effort later.'

27. [**strong.** So in Ff. 1 and 2; Ff. 3 and 4 read 'strange', to which Rosalind's reply would be perhaps even more appropriate than to 'strong'.
But this does not justify change.]

32. **dearly.** 'Dear' was used of any emotion that touches us closely,
whether love or hate; cf. 'dearest foe', *Hamlet*, ɪ. ii. 182.

34. **Why should I not ?** Many editors, following Capell, have
omitted 'not', making Celia reply: Why should I hate him ? Isn't
he a deserving young man ? This makes obvious sense, but too
obvious. It is much more in tone with Celia's gently ironic attitude
here to make her say, teasingly, as F. does: But why shouldn't I
hate him ? Doesn't he well deserve—to be hated, her tone implies.
Rosalind quickly turns Celia's words into their literal meaning:
Let me love him then, because he is well-deserving.

50. purgation. There were two kinds of legal 'purgation': (a) Canonical, the affirmation on oath of the accused's innocence, and (b) Vulgar, which required in addition ordeals by fire, water, or combat.

68. I was too young. This clearly implies that Rosalind's father had been banished long ago and had passed many years in exile: see II. i. 2. But contrast I. i. 93–114, where Oliver and Charles discuss the situation as recent. The likeliest explanation is simply that Shakespeare did not bother to be consistent.

72. Juno's swans. The swans draw Venus' chariot, not Juno's (Ovid, *Metamorphoses*, x). Shakespeare's slip passed unnoticed by his various editors and commentators until Aldis Wright's edition, the Clarendon, in 1877.

93. No, hath not? Celia repeats and queries Rosalind's 'hath not'.

99. [change. F. 2 reads 'charge', which has been adopted with obvious appropriateness, by many editors. But 'change', meaning reverse of fortune, also makes good sense.]

101. pale: not, as has been argued, the noun 'pale', meaning limit, hence extremity. Celia says that the heavens are pale in sympathy with their sorrows.

113. suit me . . . like a man. Such disguises were easier, and an obviously useful device, in Elizabethan times when boys or young men took the women's parts. On the modern stage Rosalind-Ganymede has an unhappy way of looking like the principal boy in a pantomine—Dick Whittington without his cat.

119. that . . . semblances. They escape from a difficult situation by putting on a bold front.

122. Ganymede. Lodge had already used this name for the disguised Rosalind. Ganymede was cupbearer to Jupiter (Gk. Zeus) in classical mythology.

125. Aliena. This name also Shakespeare found in Lodge, where Alinda, i.e. Celia, on fleeing to the forest, appropriately adopts it in exchange for her own: fem. of Lat. *alienus,* not one's own (opposite of *suus*).

129. He'll go . . . with me. Shakespeare insists on the devotion of Touchstone, the man inside the motley; and this devotion adds nobility to the character of Celia because she is capable of inspiring it.

**134. [F. 1 has 'go in we', with 'content' as an adjective; F. 2 has 'go we in', with 'content as a noun. The second seems the likelier meaning.]

ACT II. SCENE I

The Second Act brings us to the Forest of Arden and the true setting of the play. In this lovely pastoral and sylvan scene the little band of exiles are cheerful and even gay: some, like the Duke, finding there a philosophic content; others, like Amiens, genuinely happy; one, Jaques, watching with cynical interest the unchanging ways of man in a world very different from the larger one he has left. Arden has laid its spell on them, as on all who enter it. But theirs is a gentle adversity, beyond the reach of poverty or the need to work, however cold the winter winds may blow. They are in holiday mood; they have escaped for a time from the demands of the world to which they belong and to which they must return. The picture is not complete till the younger generation come on the scene; still more, the true rustics, who must live their lives and die there.

1. **exile.** Shakespeare accents this word on either the first or the second syllable; here the second.

5. **not the penalty of Adam.** The reading 'but the penalty of Adam', first suggested by Theobald two hundred years ago, has been very generally adopted ever since. But it is a sound principle to accept the Folio or Quarto readings when they can possibly be made to yield sense, and Theobald's emendation robs the speech of some of its point. The Duke's argument is that adversity has its advantages: they are better in Arden than at Court, for in Arden they have only natural ills instead of artificial ones, and compensating benefits. Lines 5–11 may therefore be interpreted as follows: Are not our sufferings here those common to all men living a natural life, as distinct from the sophisticated life of Courts? The most obvious of these, the change of seasons, such as the bitter cold of winter, hurts my body, but strengthens my mind, for it does not flatter me, as courtiers do, into the belief that I, a Duke, am superior to my fellow-men. Instead, it makes me feel our common humanity. On this interpretation 'Here feel we not the penalty of Adam?' is a rhetorical question like 'Hath not old custom . . . pomp?' and 'Are not these woods . . . court?' This third question then runs easily into an example of 'the penalty of Adam', and the 'sweet use' of such 'adversity' to one nursed and protected in the artificial conditions of a Court.

These lines (5–11) are difficult to punctuate satisfactorily; but it must be remembered that they are written in the free flow of Shakespeare's dramatic verse, and the exact meaning and quick change of syntax, not easily rendered in print, were meant to be conveyed by the inflection of the actor's voice.

[Much discussion has raged round 'the penalty of Adam'. The natural reference would be, of course, to the curse of toil laid upon him: 'In the sweat of thy face shalt thou eat bread' (Gen. iii. 19). But the Duke is not saying that they are lucky because they have not to work; his point is the ills they share with all the sons of Adam, not those from which they are, by virtue of their rank, exempt. Others have argued that it refers specifically to 'the seasons' difference', the change, with the Fall of Adam, from the eternal springtime of Eden (see *Paradise Lost*, Book X, ll. 651–719). But Shakespeare seems to be using the phrase with a more general significance, to cover all the natural, especially physical, ills of mankind.]

13. the toad, ugly and venomous. Since Pliny it has been a popular belief that the toad is poisonous. Shakespeare may have read of it in Holland's translation of Pliny's *Natural History*, Book 25, p. 231, which also, p. 434, mentions a bone in the right side of the toad as having many powerful qualities. The 'precious jewel' in the toad's head is apparently a combination of this bone with the medieval belief that a product made from the brains of a newly killed toad was a certain antidote against poison, and with the rock called toadstone from its colour and mottled appearance.

18. [I would not change it. F. gives this sentence to Amiens. The majority of editors, since Upton suggested it in 1746, have given it to the Duke, mainly on the ground that it rounds off his speech rhythmically and logically. But does it? The remark is, if anything, too light and free a close to the sermonizing of the Duke, and there seems no sufficient reason to take it away from that slight but attractive character, the singer Amiens.]

20. style. Amiens continues the metaphor of 'translate' (l. 19); i.e. the Duke can turn their misfortunes into sources of happiness.

26. Jaques. The pronunciation of Jaques' name has always given trouble. It was well known as a monosyllable (Jākes) in Shakespeare's time, particularly in Warwickshire. According to Mrs. Cowden-Clarke's *Concordance* it occurs sixteen times in his plays. The arguments for a dissyllable are chiefly metrical, but the name mostly (10 times out of 16) occurs in prose or at the end of a line. The remaining six instances are inconclusive, as here, where it is just possible to read it as a monosyllable. The bulk of evidence is in favour of that, but, partly because 'Jakes' is harsh in sound, there is an established convention of pronouncing the name 'Jāquez'.

31. antique: the accent on the first syllable, as usual.

38. tears. Deer were supposed to weep when dying: there is a marginal note to Drayton's *Polyolbion*, xiii, l. 160: 'The Hart weepeth at his dying: his teares are held to be precious in medicine.'

40. fool. The word is used elsewhere by Shakespeare as a term of pity or endearment, with no idea of stupidity, the most famous instance being in *Lear*, v. iii. 307, where Lear, speaking of Cordelia, says: 'And my poor fool is hang'd.'

55–7. Sweep on . . . bankrupt there ? The contempt of the Court for the City was a marked characteristic of Elizabethan London. The courtier Jaques thus finds an apt, and contemptuous, metaphor for the wounded deer abandoned by the herd in a citizen who has failed in business ('broken bankrupt') and is therefore despised and neglected by his prosperous, high-living ('fat and greasy') fellow-citizens. The rich food of City banquets was, and still is, proverbial.

59. [the country: F. 'body of country'; F. 2: 'the country'.]

62. kill . . . up. The intensive use of 'up' is still common, though not with 'kill'; cf. the slang 'beat up' for 'beat'.

ACT II. SCENE II

This short scene, in sharp contrast to the preceding one, gives a necessary jerk forward to the action of a play, the plot of which has been called, with some justification, 'lazy'. We discover the actual flight of Rosalind, Celia, and Touchstone, and the suspicion which finally brings Oliver, too, to the Forest, a moral conversion, and marriage with Celia.

13. wrestler: here a trisyllable.

ACT II. SCENE III

There is a good deal of necessary business to be got through at this stage of the play, and here Orlando is set *en route* for Arden, taking the aged Adam with him. The old serving-man turned faithful friend to his young master is a kindly contrast to some of the serving-men in Shakespeare's earlier comedies, and, although Adam has no share in the remaining action, the need to take care of him gives Orlando dignity and responsibility when he is in danger of having, from this point onwards, too little to do to sustain our interest in him.

8. bonny. There is no need to emend this, as has been done, to 'bony', with a recollection of 'sinewy' in l. 14 of the preceding scene. In Scotland and northern England 'bonny' is still used in the sense of physically fine, or even, as perhaps here, excellent in whatever quality is implied in the context. So in R. L. Stevenson's *Kidnapped*, ch. x, Alan Breck says, 'in a kind of ecstasy': 'And oh, man, am I no a bonny fighter ?'

14–15. what is comely envenoms him that bears it. This may
be suggested by the legend that the centaur Nessus, dying from
a poisoned arrow shot by Hercules, took his revenge by giving
his blood-stained tunic to Deianira, with the promise that, if she
gave it to Hercules, he would remain true to her. She innocently
did so, and the poisoned blood caused the death of Hercules. The
idea that murder could be committed by means of a poisoned
garment was not uncommon in Renaissance literature.

27. place. The word may have the meaning of mansion-house;
but here the sense is probably 'no fit place for you'.

40. foster-nurse. The idea is appropriate to a state of dependent
old age, even second childhood. For obvious reasons, Shakespeare
has made Adam a very old man (cf. 'venerable burden', II. vii.
167), dependent on the youthful vigour of the gallant Orlando.
In Lodge he is old but active.

43–4. ravens ... sparrow. See Psalm cxlvii. 9 and St. Matthew
x. 29.

50. Nor did not. Note the emphatic double negative; cf. II. iv. 8.

58. [meed: F. 'needs'; F. 2 and F. 3 'meed'.]

71. [seventeen: F. 'seventy'. Rowe made the obvious correction in his
1709 edition of Shakespeare.]

74. a week: an indefinite period of time; cf. our modern 'too late
a day'. The word is probably chosen, like 'content' in l. 68, for
the sake of the rhyming couplets. All this speech is sententious
and forced.

ACT II. Scene IV

In the Forest, as at the Court, the characters of Rosalind, Celia,
and Touchstone at once declare themselves. The fainting Celia yet
speaks gently to Corin and 'likes this place' (l. 88); Touchstone sees
that its rural solitudes are not for him (l. 13), but his irrepressible
wit breaks out in pointed jests; Rosalind courageously tackles present
and future (l. 85) difficulties. They meet the true rustics, and learn
that they, too, have their troubles, Rosalind ruefully admitting that
there is no escape from love.

1. [weary. The Folios have 'merry'; 'weary' was first adopted by
Theobald, and since then by most editors. The compositor of F. 1
may easily have read 'mery' for 'wery' in his manuscript; but it is
difficult, on dramatic grounds, to decide definitely between the two
words. The arguments for 'weary' are briefly that Touchstone catches
up Rosalind's word in his reply; that Rosalind would not proclaim
herself 'merry' in l. 1 and ready to 'cry like a woman' in l. 5; that these

opening lines are all an aside between Rosalind and Touchstone, to whom she may well confess herself 'weary' though not to the fainting Celia. For 'merry' it is argued that Touchstone may not be catching up Rosalind's word; that her opening 'O Jupiter! how merry are my spirits', is for Celia's encouragement, and her next speech, down to 'petticoat', an aside to Touchstone; that a gay courage is part of Rosalind's character.]

6. weaker vessel. See 1 Peter iii. 7: 'giving honour unto the wife, as unto the weaker vessel'.

10. cross. The Elizabethan silver penny had a double cross and a crest stamped on the reverse. There was therefore constant punning on the various meanings of the word 'cross'; 'bear one's cross' = 'bear one's trouble' (from the New Test.) and also 'carry money'.

13. Arden: perhaps a pun by pronouncing it 'a-den'.

34. [Wearing. The later Folios have 'wearying', but 'wear' and 'weary' meant, and perhaps were, the same.]

39. [thy wound. F. 1 reads 'they would'; the later Folios 'their wound'. Rowe, rightly, corrected to 'thy wound'.]

40. hard adventure. The chance hearing of Silvius reciting his pains reawakened Rosalind's: hence 'hard adventure'.

43. a-night. In this adverbial use 'a-' represents a preposition, in, on, of, as in 'aboard'.

46. wooing of a peascod. The use of a peascod as a lucky gift in rustic wooing appears in the following lines:

> 'The peascod greene oft with no little toyle
> Hee'd seek for in the fattest fertil'st soile
> And rend it from the stalke to bring it to her,
> And in her bosome for acceptance wooe her.'
> (Browne: *Britannia's Pastorals*, Bk. II, Song iii, ll. 93–6.)

Just as Touchstone says he broke his sword upon a stone, taking it for a rival, and bid him 'take that', so here he says that he wooed a peascod as an image of his lady, Jane Smile, and it is the peascod, probably the whole branch, from *whom* he took two 'cods', i.e. pea-pods, and to whom he returned them.

50. mortal. Touchstone plays on two meanings of 'mortal': the real meaning of 'subject to death' and a meaning that survives in the dialectal 'mortal' = 'exceedingly', 'very', e.g. 'mortal afraid'.

60. Holla, you clown! The 'roynish' clown of the Court takes his revenge by lording it over the clowns of the Forest.

68–9. Here's a young maid . . . succour. The meaning is clear
though the grammar faulty: understand either 'who is' before
'with travel' or 'who' before 'faints'.

74. churlish disposition. Arden is not Arcadia. Corin is poor
and must toil, for a churlish master.

88–9. [And we will mend . . . in it. F. divides these lines at 'wages'
. . . 'could' . . . 'it'. The arrangement in the text (Capell's) is much
better, in spite of the slight difficulty with 'wages'.]

ACT II. Scene V

We have already (II. i) had a glimpse, at second-hand, of Jaques,
alone in Arden, avoiding the society of his fellow exiles. He now
appears in person, reluctantly forced into their company, which he
leaves at the earliest opportunity (l. 57). Amiens' song of the
'greenwood' is a gay and charming descant on the forest life and
sweet content; but Jaques will not share in the game of make-believe,
or join these 'fools' (ll. 53 and 56) in their pretty, gallant folly. His
scepticism, however, is never allowed to mar the gracious spirit of
this part of the play. Amiens' gay courtesy survives all Jaques'
onslaughts, even the cynical parody of his song. His fellow courtiers,
in fact, do not take their 'melancholy' comrade seriously.

16. stanzo. The word was a recent importation, and Jaques ridicules
it as affected and new. So in *Love's Labour's Lost* Shakespeare
puts it into the mouth of Holofernes, the pedant.

19. names. Jaques probably means the legal signature in acknowledgement and therefore evidence of a debt. It is his bitter way
of saying that he takes no interest in the trifles that mean so much
to the singer, Amiens. His misanthropy comes out more strongly
in the next speech, in the likening of two men complimenting
each other to the meeting of two baboons.

[i' the sun. It is perhaps unnecessary to look beyond the simple and
obvious meaning, in the open air. But Hamlet's 'I am too much i'
the sun' (*Hamlet*, I. ii. 67), with its hint of exposure to danger, and the
proverbial phrase 'out of God's blessing into the warm sun' suggest
the idea of outlawry, which would apply here.]

47–54. Jaques' song. On the stage he is usually made to recite
his song; but it would give point to the parody if he affected to
sing it, with some rude, far-off imitation of Amiens' pretty trillings.

55. ducdame. This 'Greek invocation to call fools into a circle'
has been variously explained as of Latin (*duc ad me*), Italian,
French, and Celtic origin, the last from a challenging-phrase
surviving in the children's game, Tom Tidler's Ground. The latest

explanation to hold the field derives it from the Romany or Gipsy language 'dukra me', becoming 'dukda me', and meaning 'I fore-tell'. As the gipsy fortune-teller's cry, this would suit the context, and give point to Jaques' 'Greek', meaning 'a cunning person, a cheat' (*O.E.D.*), the popular notion of gipsies. This was probably what it meant to the knowing Jaques; to Amiens, as to most of those who have read or seen the play, it is mere jargon. It is a trisyllable, corresponding to 'Come hither' in scansion.

57–8. the first-born of Egypt: Exodus xi. 5. Is this a hit at Duke Senior, the 'first-born' who has brought them to the life that Jaques dislikes? Or, as Dr. Johnson thought, is it merely 'a proverbial expression for high-born persons' in general, against whom it would have been in character for Jaques to nurse a grudge?

ACT II. Scene VI

A very short scene that brings Orlando and Adam to the Forest, and shows the young man's kindness to his old and fainting charge.

ACT II. Scene VII

Jaques has made his great discovery, the superlative specimen of human folly in whom he expects to find much new matter. We get two interesting lights on the 'moralizing' Jaques in this scene. His desire to don motley and enjoy the fool's privilege in criticizing his fellows provokes a sharp rebuke from his usually amused and patient master. Jaques, we learn, has in the past lived a free, even an evil life. In the second place, Orlando's violent entry brings out the dignity of the Duke and the silent courtesy of all his followers—except Jaques, who, alone, ridicules a young man in distress (l. 90).

1. he be. The subjunctive after verbs of thinking expresses doubt: cf. 'I think my wife *be* honest and think she *is* not' (*Othello*, III. iii. 385).

6. spheres. The older astronomers imagined a series of concentric, transparent, hollow globes revolving round the earth, carrying with them the heavenly bodies—sun, moon, planets, and fixed stars. As they moved they were supposed to give out a harmonious sound which mortal ears were too dull to hear. There is a famous and beautiful reference to this music of the spheres in Milton's *Ode on the Morning of Christ's Nativity*, st. xiii.

13. a miserable world: a parenthetic exclamation. Jaques is either ridiculing his own melancholy view of life now that he has met a fool who makes him laugh, or repeating it with increased conviction since hearing the fool rail.

14–42. I met a fool . . . in mangled forms. In this description there is fully as much of Jaques as of Touchstone, who summed up his man and behaved accordingly. This is not the Touchstone whom Rosalind and Celia knew.

19. Call me not fool . . . fortune: a reference to the proverb 'Fortune favours fools'.

29. moral: probably the adjective. If the verb were intended, it would have been more natural, and equally metrical, to have written 'moralize the time'.

32. [sans. The French preposition, originally used with French words, chiefly in phrases already established in French, like sans doubt, had become practically an English word by Shakespeare's time and should be pronounced as if English.]

34–6. [A worthy fool! It is tempting to transpose the 'A' and the 'O' of ll. 34 and 36, as has been done in the new Cambridge edition, and make Jaques reply 'A worthy fool' to the Duke's question. But the change has an unnecessarily sobering effect on his, for once, excited exclaimings.]

39. dry. 'In the physiology of Shakespeare's time a dry brain accompanied slowness of apprehension and a retentive memory' (Wright). The phrase 'a dry biscuit jest' occurs in the Induction to Jonson's *Every Man Out of his Humour*.

40. places. The meaning is much as in 'common*place*-book', and the word here may cover both the topic itself and the illustration from reading and experience ('cramm'd with observation').

45. weed. The word 'suit' probably suggests 'weed', which, in the meaning of 'a garment', is often used in close conjunction with it in Shakespeare. This meaning then suggests to the poet's mind the image of the noxious plant which 'grows rank' and must be removed.

52. 'why' . . . way. The quibble is obvious and was still more obvious in Elizabethan pronunciation.

53–7. He that a fool . . . glances of the fool. 'Unless men have the prudence not to appear touched with the sarcasms of a jester, they subject themselves to his power; and the wise man will have his folly "anatomized", that is, dissected and laid open, by the "squandering glances" or random shots of a fool' (Dr. Johnson).

[F. reads: 'Doth very foolishly although he smart Seem senseless of the bob.' This might be interpreted that a wise man who receives a thrust from a fool should and does appear stupidly unaware of it however much he smarts. But metrically the line is defective, and Theobald's interpolation of 'Not to' before 'seem' is now generally accepted.]

63. counter: a small piece of thin metal, generally copper or brass, sometimes silver and even gold, used in calculations, but not current coin.

64–9. Most mischievous foul sin . . . general world. The Duke argues that, in speaking his mind about the world, Jaques, having been so great a 'libertine' himself, will accuse other men of the sins of which he has had so vast an experience. Thus he will corrupt men by 'disgorging' (l. 69) his knowledge. In his reply (l. 71) Jaques appears deliberately to misunderstand the Duke's argument by saying merely that if he attacks pride in general, no individual need think he is meant and be offended.

73. weary very means. This is almost certainly corrupt, but none of the suggested emendations are conclusive or even satisfactory. It is just possible to find a meaning in it as it stands: Does not pride flow as hugely as the sea until its very means (i.e. source of supply), being exhausted, do ebb?

95. ta'en. This word inspired Dr. Johnson to a wise and famous remark: 'We might read *torn* with more elegance, but elegance alone will not justify alteration.'

100–1. An you . . . die. Jaques' speech is difficult to read as verse, but it seems better than to suppose a fragment of prose in this verse scene.

137. This wide and universal theatre: i.e. the world. Fleay, in his *Life* of Shakespeare, suggested that this is a reference to the new Globe Theatre, completed in 1599, with its motto: 'Totus mundus agit histrionem'.

139. All the world's a stage. Earlier examples of this famous image have been sought and found. Shakespeare drew it from his profession and his own daily expérience, and it is he who has made it familiar. First the life of man is compared to that of an actor who has to play many parts in succession; then to a play with seven acts corresponding to its most marked stages.

144. mewling: echoic, like Fr. *miauler*, to mew, like a cat. From its use here, where Jaques contemptuously likens the whining cry of a baby to a cat's mew, it has acquired the human meaning.

154. capon. The capon was almost a standard present to justices of the peace from suitors or wrong-doers who wanted to influence their verdict or secure their good-will. Hence 'capon-justices' became an Elizabethan by-word.

155. beard of formal cut. The variety of fashion in which beards were cut was a favourite subject for Elizabethan satirists. The beard of a justice would be dignified ('formal'), not fantastic, in shape.

158. pantaloon. The Pantaloon, like Harlequin and Punchinello, a stock figure in popular Italian comedy, was well known to the Elizabethans. He was traditionally represented as a thin old dotard, wearing slippers, spectacles, and a pouch.

166. *Re-enter Orlando, with Adam.* This has an interest beyond its dramatic significance. The story is thus related by Steevens on the authority of the antiquarian, Oldys: 'One of Shakespeare's younger brothers, who lived to a good old age, ... would in his younger days come to London to visit his brother Will, as he called him, and be a spectator of him as an actor in some of his own plays. This custom ... he continued it seems so long after his brother's death, as even to the latter end of his own life. ... But all that could be recollected from him of his brother Will in that station was the faint, general, and almost lost ideas he had of having once seen him act a part in one of his own comedies, wherein, being to personate a decrepit old man, he wore a long beard, and appeared so weak and drooping and unable to walk, that he was forced to be supported and carried by another person to a table, at which he was seated among some company, who were eating, and one of them sung a song.' This tradition is said, not on the best authority, to have inspired Coleridge to remark: 'Great dramatists make great actors ... I am certain that he was greater as Adam, in *As You Like It*, than Burbage as Hamlet or Richard the Third. It is worth having died two hundred years ago to have heard Shakespeare deliver a single line. He must have been a great actor.' Few would share Coleridge's extravagance of feeling; and the facts, as given in this account, are certainly wrong. (Shakespeare's three brothers, for example, all died before him.) Yet it may go back to an earlier tradition in which there was some truth. If he were given the part of Adam, and if, as another story relates, his best part was the Ghost in *Hamlet*, Shakespeare seems to have been an indifferent actor. But, for what they are worth, these traditions are interesting, for they are our only glimpse, if a dubious one, of him on the stage.

177–8. Thy tooth . . . seen. A great deal has been written on why
the invisibility of the wind made its tooth less keen, and several
emendations have been made for 'seen'. Dr. Johnsᴜn, as so often,
puts Shakespeare's meaning into clear and forcible prose: 'Thy
rudeness gives the less pain as thou art not seen, as thou art an
enemy that dost not brave us with thy presence, and whose
unkindness is therefore not aggravated by insult.'

180. Heigh-ho is the traditional spelling for a sigh, but it is in fact
capable of expressing any emotion: 'an utterance apparently of
nautical origin, and marking the rhythm of movement in heaving
or hauling; often used in the burdens of songs with various
emotional expression, according to intonation' (*O.E.D.*).

ACT III. Scene I

The Third Act opens with a short but essential scene at Court, in
which the usurper Duke sends Oliver packing in search of Orlando
whom he angrily suspects of being with Rosalind and Celia (see II. ii).
It is the last of the Court scenes; Shakespeare, like his audience, is
in haste to get back to Arden.

6. Seek him with candle: a reference to Luke xv. 8, the story of
the woman searching for her lost piece of silver.

10. seize into our hands. Shakespeare takes the fact from Lodge,
but gives a different explanation. In Lodge, the usurper took the
pretext of Saladyne's (Oliver) *ill*-treatment of Rosader (Orlando)
in order to banish him, and seize his lands which he coveted.

['Seize' and 'seizure' have a strict legal sense of taking possession
after forfeiture. As there is no question of legal forfeiture here, Shakespeare is using them in a more general sense. In l. 17 'extent', too,
has a technical meaning: to make a valuation under certain legal
circumstances which do not here apply. The accuracy of Shakespeare's
legal knowledge has been often praised and as often called in question.
He is very fond of using legal terms, examples and imagery, but there
is no need to suppose, as some have done, that his undoubted familiarity
with the law can only be explained by his having been attached to it
professionally for some time, presumably as a lawyer's clerk on first
coming to London. All the evidence goes to show that he was a keen
business man, and his knowledge is not that of a professional lawyer,
like Sir Walter Scott's, but of a man who has had constant experience
of the law in transacting his affairs.]

ACT III. Scene II

This long scene is the central one of the play. Touchstone twitting
rustic simplicity, and ironically exposing the unreality of the pastoral
game that all the court-bred company are playing; Jaques' sentimental melancholy brought into disconcerting contact with real

passion; Rosalind and Orlando fathom-deep in love, but exercising their heads and tongues as well as their hearts, with Celia as an amused but sympathetic onlooker; and all this in the golden air of Arden—it is an enchanting blend of observation and poetry, wit and feeling, the high-light of Shakespeare's romantic comedy.

1–10. Hang there . . . unexpressive she. With one quatrain added after l. 8, these lines would form a Shakespearian sonnet suited to love protestation.

2. thrice-crowned. Hecate in her triple capacity is a favourite theme of poets: Hecate or Proserpina in the underworld, Luna in the sky, Diana on earth; cf. 'the triple Hecate', *Midsummer Night's Dream*, v. ii. 14. The characteristics of these three states are neatly summed up in the lines quoted by Dr. Johnson:

> 'Terret, lustrat, agit,—Proserpina, Luna, Diana—
> Ima, superna, feras, sceptro, fulgore, sagittis.'

4. Thy huntress. Orlando calls Rosalind one of Diana's huntress followers, a votaress of the virgin goddess, because, as he thinks, he has not yet won her love, and she is still fancy-free. He almost identifies her power over him with that of the 'chaste' (l. 3) moon, which sways the fates of men, as Rosalind sways his life.

13–22. Truly . . . shepherd ? Touchstone's speech is deservedly famous. It is the banished fool's comment on the privacy and peace of Arden, a corrective to the enthusiasm of the banished Duke and his courtiers. Touchstone's antitheses are far more than verbal. He has made the profound discovery that in life you cannot eat your cake and still have it, that every positive has its negative, every gain its corresponding loss.

23–30. No more . . . kindred. The old shepherd, with his humble philosophy drawn from experience, has his own, very real wisdom, as Touchstone at once recognizes (l. 31). He goes on airing and exercising his court-bred wit upon him, but the two are well-matched in their different kinds of strength, if, indeed, in ll. 71–5, Corin does not come off victor, though Touchstone naturally has the last witty word.

36–7. like an ill-roasted egg, all on one side. Corin may be something of a philosopher from his experience of the operations of nature; but he is only half-cooked, says Touchstone, not wholly in jest, from never having been at court.

64. perpend. A pompous invention which Shakespeare gives, appropriately, to Polonius, Pistol, and Touchstone.

69. incision. A metaphor from blood-letting is difficult to follow here, especially with 'raw' (l. 70). Probably, as Professor Dover Wilson suggests, it is from grafting, cf. 'incision', appropriate in speaking to a countryman.

80. **cuckoldy ram.** The word and the reproach have dropped out of polite or common usage; but the 'cuckold husband', i.e. one whose wife was unfaithful to him, used to be an unfailing jest, like the French 'le mari cocu'. The English word probably comes from the cuckoo, which lays its eggs in another bird's nest, though it is applied to the victim.

86. **Ind:** pronounced to rhyme with 'mind .

96. **rank.** This difficult word has been explained as a reference to 'riding rhyme', an early name for the heroic couplet which may come from Chaucer's Canterbury pilgrims; or as meaning row, order, file, i.e. the jog-trot way in which they ride one after another, each one as like the other as the rhymes in ll. 86–93. It seems best to keep 'rank', giving it this second meaning.

[Several conjectures and emendations have been made for 'rank': thus 'rant', meaning their volubility in selling their wares; 'rate', the shuffling pace of their horses; 'rack', a word meaning a pace between a trot and an amble.]

103. **[winter.** So in the Third Folio, the two preceding ones having 'wintred', meaning exposed to winter.]

111. **[false gallop.** 'False gallop' and 'infect' have been found coming together in a single sentence in Thomas Nashe's *Strange Newes from Parnassus*, one of the anti-Gabriel Harvey pamphlets already mentioned in the note to I. ii. 82–3. 'I would trot a false gallop through the rest of his ragged Verses, but that, if I should retort his rime dogrell aright, I must make my verses (as he doth his) run hobling like a Brewers Cart upon the stones, and observe no length in their feete, which were *absurdum per absurdius*, to infect my vaine with his imitation.' Nashe bitterly attacked Harvey's enthusiasm for classical measures in English poetry and his poor verses; and it has been argued, more or less seriously, that by putting these strong words in Rosalind's mouth, Shakespeare shows which side he espoused in this notorious quarrel. He probably did agree with Nashe, but was much more probably amused by his boisterous language; and this is all that the present passage can be taken to show.]

115–18. **I'll graff . . . medlar:** a play on the true meaning of 'medlar' and the other of a forward, interfering fellow. Touchstone, like the medlar, will go rotten before being properly ripe, i.e. has any sense.

126. **civil:** in the well-established meaning of solemn, grave, even melancholy—as in the 'sayings' that follow; though there is also a hint, as Dr. Johnson thought, of civilized reflections as opposed to those proper to the solitary forest.

129. **stretching of a span**: 'Behold, Thou hast made my days as it were a span long.' Psalm xxxix. 6 (Prayer Book Version).

137. **quintessence.** 'The "fifth essence" of ancient and medieval philosophy, supposed to be the substance of which the heavenly bodies were composed, and to be actually latent in all things'; therefore 'the purest or most perfect form or manifestation of some quality' (*O.E.D.*).

138. **in little**: explained in two ways: in miniature, or, more probably here, in the microcosm, man, as distinct from the macrocosm, the universal world.

143. **Helen's cheek.** The most beautiful woman of antiquity, Helen has become the type of womanly beauty for the western world. She was the wife of Menelaus, King of Sparta, but, during her husband's absence, was carried off by Paris, son of Priam, King of Troy. This abduction led to the ten years' Trojan War, at the end of which Troy was sacked and burned by the Greeks.

144. **Cleopatra's majesty.** Cleopatra, Queen of Egypt, became celebrated for her seductive beauty, royal bearing, extravagant excesses, learning, and cleverness. She won the love of Caesar, and, after his death, of Antony. Their passion, ruin, and death has become the most famous love story in the world: see *Antony and Cleopatra* and Dryden's interesting play, *All for Love*.

145. **Atalanta's better part.** This was the swift-footed Atalanta who, vowed to virginity, got rid of her many admirers by beating them in a race. The reward of victory was her hand in marriage; of defeat, death. Many had perished before Hippomenes outwitted her by dropping in her path three golden apples from the garden of the Hesperides given him by Venus; Atalanta stooped to pick them up, and Hippomenes arrived first at the goal. Since Dr. Johnson began it, there has been endless discussion about what Shakespeare meant by 'Atalanta's better part', which would seem, as Johnson pertinently remarked, to have been 'her heels'. Her worse part was that her success involved the death of her lovers. In all probability Shakespeare is thinking of the grace and beauty of the running girl's figure, which he must often have seen in tapestries, as well as in his mind's eye.

146. **Sad Lucretia's modesty.** Lucretia was the acknowledged type of the chaste and virtuous Roman matron. Having been treacherously ravished by Sextus, son of the tyrant Tarquin, she stabbed herself to death in the presence of her husband and father. Her death was the signal for revolution, the Tarquins were driven out, and Rome became a republic (509 B.C.).

153. **Jupiter.** This is the reading of F. The emendation 'pulpiter' has been very generally accepted, and certainly fits what immediately follows. Moreover, 'Jupiter' is not printed in italics, as proper names are in F.; but neither is 'Jove' in l. 231. The text, however, is clear; Rosalind has already appealed to Jupiter (II. iv. 1) and it sounds like the oath she would use to keep up her boyish disguise; cf. 'Ye Gods!' to-day.

172–3. **palm-tree.** In some parts of the English countryside the catkins of the goat-willow were, and are, called 'palms'. But this is Arden, where palm-trees are no more and no less likely to be found than a 'hungry lioness' (IV. iii. 126).

173. **Pythagoras' time.** Pythagoras, a Greek philosopher and mathematician of Samos in the sixth century B.C., taught that at death men's souls migrate into other creatures. Shakespeare may have found his doctrines set forth in Ovid's *Metamorphoses* (xv), a book that he seems to have known well.

174. **an Irish rat.** If Shakespeare had any particular reason for making the rat an Irish one, it has not been possible to discover it. The conquest of Ireland in Elizabeth's reign is a terrible story of savage rebellion and savage repression, of which many echoes are to be found in Spenser's *Faerie Queene* (see especially Book V), and more explicitly in his prose tract, *View of the Present State of Ireland.* To Shakespeare as to most of his English contemporaries Ireland stood for all that was wild and uncivilized, such an allusion as this was bound to raise a laugh, and that may be the sole explanation of his 'Irish rat' here; cf. later, 'Irish wolves', v. ii. 107.

180–1. **friends . . . removed:** a jesting allusion to the proverb: 'Friends may meet, but mountains never greet.' By 'friends' Celia may mean herself and Rosalind, or the lovers, Rosalind and Orlando.

190. **Good my complexion!** perhaps only an exclamation without much meaning; or a reference to Celia's 'Change you colour?' in l. 178, i.e. Do not betray me by blushing.

192–3. **One inch . . . discovery.** The contrast is between Celia's 'inch of delay' and the ocean of 'discovery', i.e. exploration, seeking, in which it will involve Rosalind, and Celia who must answer the questions she will certainly put. 'South Sea' is a reminder of the eager interest awakened by the Elizabethan voyagers.

201. **Is he of God's making?** She perhaps implies 'Or his tailor's?'

220. **Gargantua:** the legendary large-mouthed, voracious giant whom Rabelais (c. 1490–1553) had recently made proverbial.

239. [thy. F. has 'the'.]

241. [heart. F. has 'hart'.]

252. God buy you: our modern 'Good-bye'! i.e. 'God be with you', which was variously abbreviated.

265-7. You are full . . . rings. Orlando's 'pretty answers', Jaques sneeringly says, are not his own, but learned by heart from the sentimental posies, or mottoes, inscribed on rings; hence the 'goldsmiths' wives'.

268. right painted cloth. Instead of costly tapestries, rooms were often hung with cloth painted with scenes, often scriptural in subject; e.g. 'as ragged as Lazarus in the painted cloth' (*1 Henry IV*, IV. ii. 27). Short speeches were represented coming out of the mouths of the characters on labels, as in modern cartoons: Orlando says that Jaques' string of questions are as curt as these labels, and so are his replies.

271. Atalanta's heels. See note to l. 145.

294. no clock in the forest. Here, says Orlando humorously, we live by the natural time of day, measuring it by the sun; clocks belong to an artificial life. All through he seems to take this sylvan world a little less than seriously and recognize that it is not his true or lasting sphere: cf. II. vii. 112.

305. hard. 'Hard' here surely means uneasily, a slow, uneasy trot, though it has been explained as meaning that time goes so fast that the experience of seven years is compressed into seven days. 'Time goes on crutches, till love have all his rites' in *Much Ado About Nothing*, II. i. 372, seems to settle the point.

342. [half-pence. 'No halfpence were coined in Elizabeth's reign till 1582-3. . . . They all had the portcullis with a mint mark, and on the reverse a cross moline with three pellets in each angle, so that, in comparison with the great variety in coins of other denominations then in circulation, there was a propriety in saying "as like one another as halfpence are". They were used till 1601.' (Wright.)]

352. quotidian of love. Quotidian fevers were thought to be a cardinal symptom of love.

356-7. cage of rushes. Rosalind, in keeping with her pose that Orlando's love is not as real as he pretends, teasingly suggests that the bars of his prison-cage of love are merely made of rushes.

359-67. A lean cheek . . . desolation. These were, more or less seriously, regarded as the characteristic marks of a lover in Elizabethan times. Hamlet's 'stockings foul'd, ungarter'd, and down-gyved to his ancle' (*Hamlet*, II. i. 79) were taken by Polonius as sure proof that he was mad with love for Ophelia.

368. point-device. A shortened form of 'at point device', from Fr. *à point devis,* according to a carefully devised point of accuracy.

403. wash your liver. The liver was thought to be the seat of love; cf. 'spleen', IV. i. 190, and note.

ACT III. SCENE III

A comic counterpart to the romance of Orlando and Rosalind is the love-making between Touchstone and Audrey. Is it a queer attraction that draws him to the plain and stupid girl? Or is it that Touchstone means to have a love-affair like his betters, and through it mock at this strange disease of love. That is, in fact, what he does; and Jaques, who had abruptly left the romantic Orlando in disgust, stays to watch Touchstone's wooing, sure that it will provide food for his satiric humour as it does for Touchstone's own.

3–4. doth my simple feature . . . features ? The point of the jest is lost; and it is a cold business trying to recover it. What meaning is there in 'features' that makes Audrey exclaim 'Lord warrant us!' Perhaps the explanation lies in Touchstone's pronunciation of 'feature' as 'faitor'—a good contemporary pronunciation, but confusing it with this other word that meant 'rascal'. Not, as Furness says, 'a sidesplitting joke', but enough to disconcert Touchstone who was fishing for a compliment on his feature— either in our modern sense or meaning his general make-up.

6. the most capricious poet, honest Ovid. A well-known translation of Ovid, by Arthur Golding, appeared in Shakespeare's lifetime, that of the *Metamorphoses* as early as 1567; but he may have read some part of the poems in Latin. At any rate, he found them a rich source of stories and allusions. To him, as to Touchstone, Ovid is above all the poet of love, round which his fancy freely plays ('capricious'); and 'honest' is probably inspired by Ovid's genial frankness on this and most other subjects.

    Goths: F. Gothes: to be pronounced, of course, very like 'goats': a reference to Ovid's exile to the Euxine among the Getae.

8. Jove in a thatch'd house. Jove and Mercury, travelling in disguise over Asia, were welcomed in the cottage of an aged Phrygian couple, Baucis and her husband Philemon. Jove was so pleased with his reception that he changed the humble cottage into a magnificent temple, installed Baucis and Philemon as priests, and granted their request to die at the same hour. After death their bodies were turned into trees at the temple door. The story is told in Ovid's *Metamorphoses,* Book VIII, where Golding's translation describes the roof of the cottage as 'thatched all with straw and fennish reede'.

11–12. it strikes . . . room. These words very probably refer to the death of Marlowe, the circumstances of which were made known to us in some legal documents discovered by Dr. J. L. Hotson and published by him in 1925. They show that Marlowe was struck dead on 30 May 1593 in a room of Elinor Bull's tavern at Deptford Strand by one Ingram Frysar in a quarrel over 'le recknynge'. A stage reference to it would obviously have more point about the time of Marlowe's death than six or seven years later; and ll. 11–12 may possibly, therefore, have some bearing on the question of an earlier draft of *As You Like It*. On the other hand, Marlowe's *Hero and Leander* was only printed in 1598, and the quotation from it in III. v. 80–1 proves that Shakespeare was thinking of Marlowe at this later date and in this very Act. The notorious circumstances of a fellow dramatist's death must have made a deep impression on him, and he, if not his audience, was hardly likely to forget them. '*A great reckoning in a little room*' recalls Marlowe's 'Infinite riches in a little room' (*The Jew of Malta*, I. i. 37).

46. horns. The husband of an unfaithful wife was supposed to wear a horn or horns on his forehead, as a public sign of his shame. Touchstone implies (l. 54) that all married men wear this badge, in contrast to 'the bare brow of a bachelor'. The various meanings of 'horn' provided one of the hardest-worked puns on the Elizabethan stage; cf. IV. i. 58.

70. nay, pray be covered. Note Touchstone's condescension, as if he were a lord unbending to a social inferior. Jaques presumably doffed his hat for the ceremony to begin.

73. her bells. The gender is right; the male hawk was called a 'tiercel'.

86–7. Audrey . . . bawdry. The rhymes ring the close of the scene; the rest is Touchstone's nonsense as they go out. He is quoting (contradictory) scraps of an old song, and there is no point in arguing whether he means 'Yea' or 'Nay'. He is merely teasing the priest. 'Sweet' seems to have been a traditional adjective for Oliver.

ACT III. Scene IV

Here Rosalind's gay, teasing mood (as in III. ii) has disappeared, and we are shown her as a girl very much in love, uncovering her innermost fancies and longings to the trusted Celia.

7. His very hair . . . colour. Rosalind wonders if she can really

trust Orlando's professed love for 'Rosalind'. Red hair was supposed to be the sign of a false nature. In the old paintings and
tapestries Judas was represented with red hair and beard.

15. [**cast.** F. 2 has 'chast' meaning chaste. Furness holds that this is
the true reading, arguing that the idea of chastity is inseparable from
Diana. But 'bought' and 'cast' (off) agree very well.]

16. **winter's sisterhood.** The meaning is clear: a cold, unfruitful
sisterhood, because of their chastity; cf. 'a barren sister . . .
chanting faint hymns to the cold fruitless moon' (*A Midsummer
Night's Dream*, I. i. 72–3).

24. **concave . . . goblet.** Why *covered* goblet? 'It is the idea of
hollowness, not that of emptiness, that Shakespeare wishes to
convey; and a goblet is more completely hollow when covered
than when it is not' (Mason). Orlando's love, says Celia, does not
sound true and solid.

32–6. **I met the duke . . . Orlando.** Severe moralists have remarked that Rosalind is not a very dutiful daughter in neglecting
to make herself known to Duke Senior and speaking thus of their
only encounter as yet in the Forest. But Rosalind was in love;
and a greater concern for her father was not part of Shakespeare's
comic purpose.

39. **traverse.** To break a lance directly against an adversary's
breast was considered honourable; but across it dishonourable
and a sign of want of skill. Compare *Ivanhoe*, ch. viii: 'The antago-
nist of Grantmesnil, instead of bearing his lance-point fair against
the crest or shield of his enemy, swerved so much from the direct
line as to break the weapon athwart the person of his opponent,
a circumstance which was accounted more disgraceful than that
of being actually unhorsed; because the latter might happen
from accident, whereas the former evinced awkwardness and want
of management of the weapon and the horse.'

ACT III. Scene V

This scene gives yet another 'study' of love and its ways. Silvius
and Phebe are not, of course, true rustics, but the 'shepherd and
shepherdess' of pastoral, and their relationship follows a stock
pattern. The unreality of Phebe's pride is exposed by the sharp
common sense of Rosalind, who now knows the pangs of true love.

7. **dies and lives.** This suffered many curious interpretations and
conjectured readings until Arrowsmith, in *Notes & Queries*,
pointed out that it is, of course, simply an inversion of 'lives and
dies', i.e. subsists from the cradle to the grave.

22. [lean but upon: F. 1: 'lean upon'; F. 2, 3, 4: 'lean but upon', which scans better; but in F. 1 a pause after 'it' can fill out the line.]

37. no beauty. We expect 'though you have *some* beauty', in view of l. 40; but l. 42 confirms the reading. Rosalind is being sarcastic.

39. dark to bed: sarcastic again: *Your* beauty is not worth a light to see it by.

46-8. 'Tis not . . . worship. Fair beauty was more fashionable than dark in Elizabethan times, perhaps because the Queen was fair, though the tradition goes back at least to the Middle Ages (see, e.g., the description of the fair Emelye in Chaucer's *Knight's Tale*, ll. 177-92). These lines recall the Dark Lady of Shakespeare's *Sonnets*: see *Sonnets* CXXX and CXXVII:

> 'In the old age black was not counted fair,
> Or if it were, it bore not beauty's name.'

53. That . . . children: i.e. by being determined to marry one so plain as Phebe—another lash to her vanity.

66. your. There is no need to change the F. 'your' to 'her', as many have done, if we suppose that Rosalind addresses the first part of her sentence to Phebe, the second to Silvius.

73. Besides . . . house. This can be read as a five-foot line, not an Alexandrine, if 'Besides' is treated as one syllable, quickly slurred over, and 'you will' is spoken 'you'll'; cf. l. 117.

74. tuft of olives. Shakespeare found this clump of un-English trees in Lodge.

80-1. Dead . . . sight? The 'saw' is from the poem *Hero and Leander*, 1st Sestiad, l. 177, by Marlowe (see note to III. iii. 11-12). The exclamation 'Dead shepherd' gives a hint of Shakespeare's regret for the untimely end of his fellow-poet; and the words are especially appropriate in the mouth of the shepherdess, Phebe, for in the long tradition of pastoral poetry the shepherds piped as they watched their flocks, and 'shepherd' became a hallowed name for poet; cf. the lovely use of the tradition in Milton's *Lycidas*.

122. constant . . . damask. Roses and fabrics came from Damascus, which gave its name to both. Does Shakespeare mean that the particular rose called 'damask' differs from the 'constant red' of other roses in being 'mingled' red and white? Our damask rose is pink. *Sonnet* CXXX has

> 'I have seen roses damask'd, red and white,
> But no such roses see I in her cheeks;'—

which would suggest mingled, patterned in sheen or colour like the fabric damask.

ACT IV. Scene I

Rosalind shows no more patience with the 'melancholy' Jaques than Orlando did (III. ii). The love-scene that follows his exit is a kind of implicit criticism of Jaques' contempt for love and youthful happiness.

18. [**in which my often rumination:** F. 1: 'in which by often rumination'; F. 2: 'my' for 'by'. Editors have hesitated between omitting 'in', retaining 'by', and retaining 'in' and accepting 'my' from F. 2.]

31-6. **Farewell ... gondola.** The travelled Englishman who came back affecting to be too refined for his native speech and national habits was a favourite subject of sixteenth-century writers. The best-known attack on the more deeply corrupting influence of a stay in Italy (l. 36) is in Roger Ascham's *Scholemaster*; but the 'Englishman Italianate' was a by-word.

43. [**thousandth:** F. 'thousand'; the ordinal '-th' was recent in Shakespeare's day, and this spelling may indicate the pronunciation, like 'sixt' for 'sixth'.]

79. **of my suit.** 'Out' must be remembered from l. 75: so 'out of my suit'. There is a quibble on the two meanings of 'suit': (i) lover's pleading and (ii) apparel (l. 80).

90. **Grecian club.** All the authorities say by the sword or spear of Achilles; Rosalind teasingly invents the 'club', like Leander's 'cramp' in l. 95, in order to belittle those famous 'patterns of love' (l. 91), who have died, 'but not for love', she says, for no *man* knows how to love. Men always die of something else.

96. [**chroniclers.** Many editors emend 'chroniclers' to 'crowners' (coroners) who 'find' tne verdict that 'Hero of Sestos' caused Leander's death. But it is an unlikely change for a compositor to make, and 'chroniclers' makes equally good sense, perhaps better.]

119-20. **a girl ... priest:** i.e. a girl (who) anticipates the question which the priest (Celia) should have asked; i.e. Will you, Rosalind, have to husband this Orlando?

129-31. **I will be ... hen.** The 'barb' or Barbary pigeon apparently has no special reputation of this kind, but the adjective conveys a sufficient hint of Oriental jealousy, as we might speak jestingly of 'a sheik'.

132. [**new-fangled.** The adjective is originally 'newfangel', as in Chaucer; the '-d' is a late addition, as if the word were a (past) participial adjective.]

133-4. **Diana in the fountain.** A figure, with water so conveyed through it that it appeared to weep, was a favourite design for a fountain, and the figure was often of Diana.

135. **hyen.** It was a popular notion that the bark of the hyena was like a loud laugh.

146. **Wit, whither wilt?** A common phrase, apparently proverbial; cf. 1. ii. 52–3. It might be, originally, a jesting way of saying that there is no wit in present company.

151–2. **You . . . tongue.** A woman's ready tongue was proverbial then as now. See Chaucer's *Merchant's Tale*, l. 2265 et seq. for an account of Proserpine's vow to Pluto that henceforth she will give every woman the power to have an answer ready to anything, especially to any charge a man may bring.

163. **'tis but one cast away, and so, come, death!** Rosalind's pretty exaggeration sounds like a quotation from a song.

167–8. **oaths that are not dangerous.** If this is, as some have (quite unnecessarily) thought, a reference to the statute passed in 1605 against blasphemy on the stage, then it must be a late insertion in the play. But Rosalind probably means the kind of oath which, as a girl in man's disguise, she might—and does—safely speak.

170. **pathetical.** Literally passionate or passion-moving, this word seems here to be more loosely used, parallel to 'hollow'; cf. modern slang use of 'pathetic'=awful, of anything that inspires a half-pitying contempt.

178. **let Time try.** 'Time tryeth Troth' was a favourite motto for rings and sundials.

181–2. **the bird . . . nest.** Shakespeare found this reference to the proverbial bird that fouls its own nest in Lodge.

186. **the bay of Portugal.** This was the name given by sailors to the sea off the coast of Portugal from Oporto to Cintra, where the Atlantic was deep. Elizabethan London was thronged with sailors, and Shakespeare was familiar enough with the nautical terms of the 'sea-dogs', and with their picturesque talk of strange places and adventures.

189. **wicked . . . Venus:** the blind boy Cupid, the tricky young god of love.

190. **thought.** This has the idea of melancholy fancy. In this sense it is not uncommon in Shakespeare's time, and in the allied sense of care, anxiety, as in the phrase 'to take thought for the morrow'.

spleen. In the old physiology the spleen was thought to be the seat of melancholy, anger, and ill temper.

ACT IV. Scene **II**

This little scene is interesting. It is an interruption to an audience that wants to know what happens when Orlando keeps his appointment with Rosalind. But dramatically it is necessary to suggest the lapse of time, the 'two hours' of their parting (IV. i. 155). Shakespeare's dealings with time are always interesting. No member of his audience, of course, ever supposes that the eighteen lines of this scene occupy two hours. It is sufficient that Shakespeare succeeds in suspending our sense of 'real' time, and leading us, by suggestion, into another time dimension, that of ideal or imagined or, as it is sometimes called, dramatic time.

3–5. **Let's present him . . . victory.** Jaques is fooling the triumphant 'foresters', but it was the custom in the sixteenth century so to present those who had been foremost in the chase: cf. 'To them which in this huntynge do showe moste prowess and actyvyty, a garlande or some other lyke token to be given in sign of victory, and with a joyful manner to be broughte in the presence of hym that is chiefe of the company there, to receive condigne prayse for their good endeavour' (Sir Thomas Elyot: *The Boke of the Governour*, 1531, Bk. I, ch. xviii).

6. **forester.** Jaques' words clearly imply that the 'forester' is the customary singer of the party, i.e. almost certainly Amiens, whom he ironically calls 'forester' because of his garb and present occupation; it is in character for him to harp on his companions' pretence to follow this woodland craft.

8–9. **Sing . . . enough.** Jaques is being ironical again at Amiens' expense, but this and the previous scene (II. v) suggest that he may, in fact, have taken pleasure in Amiens' singing.

10–18. [**What shall . . . scorn.** Music was set to this song, as a round for four basses, by John Hilton, organist of St. Margaret's, Westminster (1599–1657), whose setting further complicates a problem already difficult in the text. 'The rest shall bear this burden' is clearly a stage direction, and omitted in Hilton's setting. But he also omits 'Then sing him home'; and this has suggested to musicians that these words, and these words only, are the 'burden', which would not fit into a round. But, when the text only is considered, it has been variously argued that the 'burden' is ll. 10–12 (repeated at the end); or, alternatively, ll. 13–18; or, ll. 13–14 and 17–18. This seems to leave the poor soloist little pre-eminence, but perhaps that is right, for the words demand that all should join in lusty, rollicking song. As to its details, in the absence of the original setting, there can be no finality about the possible permutations and combinations; and Shakespeare would have been the first to say, 'Sing it *as you like it*'.]

18. *Exeunt.* Can Jaques possibly have refrained from giving a further ironic comment on the 'noise' (l. 9) when he has heard it? It has been suggested that some words may have been lost here, either 'cut' on the stage, or dropped by the printer. It is more likely that the band are supposed to go out singing, their voices dying away in the distance, while the connoisseur, Jaques, shows his verdict by expressive look and gesture.

ACT IV. SCENE III

After a short episode in which Rosalind once more tries to open Silvius's eyes to Phebe's silliness, the action of the play suddenly moves swiftly, when Oliver relates how Orlando has saved his life, and how he is a changed man in consequence. Celia at once falls in love with the penitent; but the high dramatic point of the scene is Rosalind's swoon on hearing that Orlando has been wounded.

2. **much.** Rosalind is speaking ironically.

7. **[did.** Many editors omit 'did', as in F. 2. But Phebe may be a monosyllable here and in v. iv. 21.]

17. **as rare as phœnix.** 'That there is but one Phoenix in the World, which after many hundred years burneth itself, and from the ashes thereof ariseth up another, is a conceit not new or altogether popular, but of great Antiquity' (Sir Thomas Browne: *Vulgar Errors*, Book III, ch. xii).

'Od's my will: one of Rosalind's 'oaths that are not dangerous' (IV. i. 167–8), but more vigorous than her wont, for she is angry.

27. **housewife's hand:** i.e. rough and worn, unfit to pen a letter which is charming enough, though Rosalind scorns it.

34. **giant-rude:** quite a characteristic Shakespearian compound, meaning rude like a giant, with a gigantic rudeness.

35. **Ethiop.** For the blackness of the 'Ethiop', compare *Romeo and Juliet*, I. v. 49–50:

'she hangs upon the cheek of night
Like a rich jewel in an Ethiop's ear.'

49. **Meaning me a beast.** Rosalind says: By contrasting me with the eye of *man*, she means that I am a beast. Phebe, of course, meant that Ganymede was a god (ll. 40 and 44).

53. **aspect.** In the old astrology, aspect meant the favourable or unfavourable appearance of the planets. The accent is on the second syllable.

70. a tame snake. Love, that is, has stolen all his resistance, robbed him of his venom.

75. fair ones. Celia is apparently the only woman, but both are young and fair (cf. l. 85).

87. a ripe sister. Ganymede, that is, seems to treat Aliena with the tenderness and care of an elder sister for a younger one.

100. an hour. 'Two hours' in IV. i. 155. Oliver—or Shakespeare—has made a mistake.

101. [food. The word is sometimes altered to 'cud', and often so misquoted. 'Cud' is apparently due to Scott, who, in the *Introduction to Quentin Durward*, makes the Marquis de Hautlieu say that he loves to sit, . . . 'Showing the code of sweet and bitter fancy.' Scott continues: 'Against this various reading of a well-known passage in Shakespeare I took care to offer no protest; for I suspect Shakespeare would have suffered in the opinion of so delicate a judge as the Marquis, had I proved his having written "chewing the cud," according to all other authorities.' Thus popular mis-quotations are formed. In fact, no 'authority' seems to have suggested 'cud' until Scott's capacious memory—stored full, as his prose constantly reveals, of Shakespeare's phrases—led him into the slip. The line, in his own version of it, was a favourite with him; see, e.g., *Journal*, 13 May 1827.]

118. To prey . . . dead. It is often said and thought that a lion will not attack a dead man, or one who feigns to be dead.

125. to Orlando. Celia's interest, already, is in the brother, Oliver, ll. 121, 133, 134; Rosalind's in Orlando, here and in l. 138.

142. In brief. This, taken with 'recountments', the plural, in l. 140, has led some to suppose that here a few lines have been dropped by the printer, or that Shakespeare has 'cut' Oliver's speech. An alternative suggestion is that Oliver himself has 'cut' his story, either overcome by his own emotion or in response to Rosalind's evident impatience.

155. [his: F. 1 'this': F. 2, 3, 4 'his'.]

159. Cousin. At this moment of excitement, Celia forgets her role of 'sister', but at once recovers it with 'Ganymede'.

165–80. I do so . . . Will you go? Momentarily overcome by Orlando's danger, Rosalind's undaunted spirit appears delightfully in the closing lines of this scene, when, even as she grows 'paler and paler', she bids Oliver commend her 'counterfeiting' to Orlando. When she next meets Orlando she at once reminds him that her faint was 'counterfeit' (v. ii. 25). Rosalind will be gallant and lively to the end, and we can safely prophesy that Orlando will never be bored in his wife's company.

ACT V. SCENE I

Shakespeare takes an amused interest in displaying Touchstone's wooing, and the queer attraction that links his fate with Audrey.

4. old gentleman. To Audrey, Jaques is an 'old gentleman'; he seems rather to be middle-age incarnate.

16–17. Cover . . . covered. Touchstone once more takes a tone of courtesy and lordly condescension; cf. III. iii. 70, and note.

31–4. The heathen . . . open. William's mouth is gaping open, and Touchstone hints that Audrey is not a grape for his eating. The mention of the 'heathen philosopher' is not to be taken as a true reference, any more than the 'figure in rhetoric' (l. 40). Touchstone means to bamboozle the simple rustic, as in ll. 39–56, with this elaborate talk. It is 'merry' enough, as the dull William dimly feels (l. 59); but perhaps the cream of the jest is when Audrey, who has probably understood no more than his last word 'depart', adds, in an important tone, her 'Do, good William', and William promptly takes his bewildered departure.

ACT V. SCENE II

By this stage in the play there is little time left for the poetry or the expansive flow of witty talk of earlier scenes. There are loose threads to be tied, and Shakespeare proceeds to tie them.

7. [her. F. 1: 'nor sudden consenting'; Rowe inserted the necessary 'her'.]

18. sister. Oliver enters into the game by treating Ganymede as Rosalind, the 'sister', not 'brother', of his future wife, Aliena.

28–39. Nay . . . part them. In this play love is at first sight, with all the romance and mysterious excitement with which Shakespeare can invest it. It is not his way to provide sober motives for this fine frenzy, as Lodge has done. In the novel, Saladyne is a reformed character before coming to the forest, and wins his way to Aliena's heart by rescuing her from a brutal attack by a band of ruffians. The giving of Celia to the once-murderous Oliver has seemed to many, including Swinburne, the one serious blot on the play; but this is surely taking it too literally.

30. thrasonical: from the name of a braggart soldier, Thraso, in Terence's *Eunuchus*.

30–1. I came . . . overcame: Caesar's famous epigram, *Veni, vidi, vici*, describing his conquest over Pharnaces in one day.

39. clubs. This was the weapon and the cry of the London apprentices in their frequent street fights: see *The Fortunes of Nigel,* ch. 1. It was also the cry to summon officers to part the com· batants, and this is the meaning here.

41. nuptial. Shakespeare uses both the singular and the plural forms of the word.

57–9. I have ... damnable. Orlando must have thought Rosalind's early teachers a strange mixture: first, 'an old religious uncle' taught her to speak (III. ii. 332); now, since she was three years old, she 'conversed with a magician', who taught her his magic, but not diabolic, arts. This guarded claim to a beneficent ('not damnable') magic power is probably a reference to the Elizabethan Act against 'Conjuracons, Inchantmentes, and Witchecraftes', which enacted heavy punishment for those convicted of witchcraft.

64. human: i.e. not a phantom, but in her human person.

91–3. [observance ... obeisance. In F. 1 the last word of l. 93 is, again, 'observance' as in l. 91. The compositor has inadvertently copied he word; 'obeisance', like 'obedience', 'endurance', 'deservance', which have all been suggested, is a mere guess.]

105. To her ... hear. Note the dramatic irony. The audience (and Rosalind) know that she is here though Orlando does not.

107. Irish wolves. Wolves howling at the moon is a perfect image of melancholy and desolation; but Rosalind is rather insisting here on the monotonous reiteration of their cry—and of the last speeches. The comparison occurs in Lodge, but in another sense and context, that of the hopeless beseeching of a lady by her lover; and the wolves are 'of Syria'. Is there anything more particularly appropriate of 'Irish wolves' than of 'an Irish rat' (III. ii. 174 and note)? Wolves survived later in Ireland than in England, but this is hardly an explanation. Among many strange stories about the little-known inhabitants of Ireland was the legend that once a year they were changed into wolves; and this might be the point of the allusion if it were immediately caught by an Elizabethan audience. For us, however, the point, if there be one, is now lost.

ACT V. Scene III

Like Act IV, sc. ii, this short scene conveys the lapse of time, and gives the excuse for bringing in one of the prettiest songs in Shakespeare.

To suit the youthful singers its theme is the springtime of man and
of the year; and it has the real feeling of the country better than all
the Duke's moralizing. Touchstone and Audrey, who were rightly
absent while the romantic lovers plighted their troth in the previous
scene, now, in comic contrast, echo these vows; and the difference
in humour between Touchstone and Jaques is seldom better seen
than in their response to song (see II. v and IV. ii).

4-5. a woman of the world. Audrey wants to be married, and, as
a matron, enjoy a fuller experience and be allowed by convention
to move more freely in the world, than as a maid. 'A woman of
the world' and 'Audrey' are incongruous terms; but female longing
since the beginning of time is compressed into her wish.

9. sit i' the middle. Touchstone sits between the two boys, and
joins in the refrain while, perhaps, Audrey looks on in stolid
wonder at this incomprehensible masculine glee.

15. *Song.* There is a setting to this delightful song in Thomas
Morley's *First Book of Airs or little short songs* (1600), which has
been described as 'the ideal of what a Shakespearian setting ought
to be'.

29-31. [And therefore . . . prime. F. 1 has this as the second stanza of
the song; it should clearly be the last, and is always thus printed.]

35. untuneable. Unlike Feste, the fool in *Twelfth Night*, Touchstone
is no musician, and his pose as a knowing musical critic is part of
the fun of this happy scene. Objection has been made to 'untuneable', in the light of the page's answer: 'we kept time'. But perhaps, as Wright points out, the page misunderstands him in order
to give Touchstone an opening for another joke.

ACT V. Scene IV

Much criticism has been levelled against this scene. The action
is huddled; the Masque of Hymen is forced and unnecessary, and
its language so unlike Shakespeare's that it is generally supposed
to be a stage interpolation by some other writer; the appearance of
Jaques de Boys is dramatically unlikely. (Shakespeare simply took
it from Lodge.) Against these and other points of complaint there
is little need to defend him. His play is done, and his main concern
now is to get all his actors happily off the stage. But he still has
time for a last glimpse of Touchstone and Jaques in an encounter
of wit, and a gay epilogue in which Rosalind exploits her double sex.

4. As those . . . fear: i.e. as those who are afraid that they are only
hoping (= that their hopes have no reality) and are certain of
nothing but that they fear.

21. [you: As in F. 'Phebe' may be a monosyllable here as in IV. iii. 7.]

32. desperate: a reference to the belief that workers in magic
bargained to sell their souls to the Devil, despairing of salvation.

43-6. I have trod . . . one. These, according to Touchstone, are
the marks of a courtier.

49. the seventh cause. In spite of ll. 64–5, Dr. Johnson argued
that it should be 'not the seventh cause', according to Touchstone's
series in ll. 66–92. If he 'durst go no further than the "lie
circumstantial"' (ll. 81–2), then that is the sixth in his series.
But we cannot press the fool's argument too closely or expect
his verbal quips to be consistent.

56-7. A poor . . . own. This has become one of the commonest of
all Shakespearian misquotations: A poor thing, but mine own.

62. the fool's bolt. The proverb ran: A fool's bolt is soon shot.

63. dulcet diseases. Many conjectures have been made about
the true reading of this: e.g. 'discourses', 'sayings', 'phrases'.
Touchstone knows his business as a clown, and is not so particular
to be exact in meaning and expression as his critics. The contrast,
too, between 'dulcet' and 'diseases' is very like the verbal quib-
bling which was his profession, and which becomes more marked
in this scene where he is once again addressing courtiers.

66-7. bear . . . seeming. It is not necessary to argue, as some have
done, that Touchstone becomes ashamed of his 'ill-favoured
thing' when he sees her in courtly company. It amuses him to
fire words and ideas at Audrey that she cannot understand.

83. measured swords. Measuring swords was the first preliminary
to the actual duel, to make sure that neither duellist had the
advantage in length.

86. the book. The 'book' might have been one of several which
laid down the code of honourable duelling for the Elizabethan
gallant. But in general terms these formal distinctions were
well known—otherwise Touchstone's jesting would miss fire—and
it is doubtful if he is drawing on any 'book' in particular.

[Elizabethan treatises on duelling mostly derived, in some degree, from an Italian work, Girolamo Muzio's *Il Duello* (1551). The likeliest is a translation of another Italian book, Vincentio Saviolo's *Practise of the Rapier and Dagger* (1595); the *Booke of Honor and Armes* (1590), probably by Sir William Segar, Norroy Herald, also drew material from Muzio, and *Paradoxes of Defence* (1599), by George Silver, contained a summary of the laws Muzio had laid down. Touchstone, however, does not keep closely to any one of these. Saviolo's 'book' has five 'lies' to his two: the 'lie circumstantial' and the 'lie direct'; its 'lie conditional' is practically the same as his joke about 'if'.

87. books for good manners. Furnivall has edited many of these in his delightful *The Babees Book* (Early English Text Society, No. 32). They described, in great detail, the perfect manners for a gentleman, especially a fine gentleman. The education of fine ladies, though not forgotten, received less attention.

104. *Enter Hymen.* The Masque of Hymen is totally unprepared for in what goes before, and is, most critics are agreed, an interpolation by some other hand than Shakespeare's, between 1600 and the publication of the First Folio in 1623. During the reign of James I, masques became extremely popular, the most famous being those in which Ben Jonson collaborated with Inigo Jones.

110–11. That thou . . . is. This, the F. 2 reading, means: that thou might'st join her (Rosalind's) hand, whose heart is already within Orlando's bosom (since she has given it to him), with his hand.

[F. 1 reads:

> That thou might'st join his hand with his,
> Whose heart within his bosom is.

The pronouns here have given some trouble. F. 2 reads: her hand; and Malone, accepting this, proposed also to read: her bosom; but this is perhaps too clear for such a speech. It is just possible that F. 1 is right, and that the masculine pronouns are a reminder of the masculine form under which Rosalind had been wooed by Orlando.]

115. [sight. There is no need to change, with Dr. Johnson, 'sight' to 'shape' in order to agree with Phebe's 'sight and shape' in l. 116.]

144. Even daughter. The interpretation of this phrase depends on whether we think it addressed to Rosalind or to Celia. If to Celia, the Duke is saying that she is no less welcome than a daughter; if to Rosalind, that she is no less welcome than a daughter should be. The passage is so forced, and unlike Shakespeare even when he is most difficult, that one can hardly believe it is his.

147. *Enter Jaques de Boys.* The Stage Direction in F. is merely 'Second Brother'; see note to I. i. 5.

164–5. To one ... potent dukedom. If scrutinized by readers who persist in demanding strict accuracy from Shakespeare, these lines are not wholly clear in cold print. Who gets back 'his lands with-held' (l. 164) and who the 'potent dukedom' (l. 165)? The first is certainly Oliver, whose lands were confiscated by the usurping Duke (III. i. 10 and note), and who now, conveniently for himself and Shakespeare, forgets that he had recently (v. ii. 10–12) sworn to hand over all his lands and greatness to Orlando and live and die a shepherd with Celia in Arden. This interpretation is supported by l. 185, and proved by Lodge's novel, at the end of which Gerismond (Duke Senior) 'restored Saladyne to all his father's lande'. The 'other', who gets 'a land ... a potent dukedom', is thus Orlando, who, by marrying Rosalind, becomes heir to her father's restored Dukedom. Once more, the proof is in Lodge, where Gerismond 'by the consent of his nobles created Rosader heire apparant to the kingdom'. Shakespeare often, in his easy, masterly way, takes the facts of his source and changes or does not bother to give their explanation; cf. III. i. 10 and note, and v. ii. 28–39 and note. Here he is winding up his play so as to make everything as pleasant as possible for everyone, and what he gives is sufficient to make us feel, in the theatre, that 'earthly things made even atone together'.

170–1. Shall share ... states. Since Act II, sc. vii, Shakespeare has forgotten the faithful Adam, who in Lodge was made Captain of the King's Guard, and Corin, the Master of Celia's Flocks; but they, presumably, are also among the 'happy number', and share in the general rewarding. Shakespeare, as Dr. Johnson often pointed out, was in a hurry to end his play.

180–1. To him ... learn'd. Still pursuing the matter that will feed his 'humour', as all this good-will and happiness certainly does not, Jaques decides to seek the 'convertite' Duke, as once he had sought the 'material fool' (III. iii. 28).

182. bequeath. The word is right in the mouth of one taking leave of the world.

183. deserves: two subjects, as often in Shakespeare, with a singular verb, perhaps because the verb 'agrees with the nearest subject', but more probably because the two subject nouns stand for different things or ideas, and are thought of as separate.

187–8. And you ... victual'd. This unkind legacy may foreshadow the probable sequel to Touchstone's unequal match, or merely express Jaques' annoyance because Touchstone, too, has left him

to rail alone at mortal happiness. Some have argued that Touchstone and Audrey are fully as likely to enjoy a long and happy
married life as the more romantic lovers.

192. *Exit.* To adapt to Jaques Dr. Johnson's famous comment on
'Exit Pistol' (*Henry V*, v. i. 94): 'I believe every reader regrets
his departure.'

EPILOGUE. After the Restoration, when female parts were no
longer played by boys but by women, it became quite 'the
fashion to see the lady the epilogue'. The actresses Nell Gwynne
and Mrs. Bracegirdle became noted for their skill in making this
difficult closing address to the audience.

197. **good wine needs no bush.** This has come to mean that it
needs no advertising, which is Rosalind's meaning here. The
proverb derives from the practice of hanging an ivy-bush as an
inn-sign, because, it has been suggested, of the association of ivy
with Bacchus, but much more probably because a cup or funnel
of ivy-wood was thought to have the power of separating wine
from the water with which inn-keepers diluted it. The ivy-bush
was therefore a sign of the purity of the wine sold within the inn.

208–9. **If I were a woman.** Pepys is excellent and interesting authority for the change from boys to women in female parts after the
Restoration. 'January 3, 1661. To the Theatre, where was acted
"Beggar's Bush"; and here the first time that ever I saw women
come upon the stage.' Later, 'Feb. 12, 1661. By coach to the
Theatre, and there saw "The Scornful Lady", now done by a
woman, which makes the play appear much better than ever it
did to me.' The new custom quickly established itself.

SELECT LITERARY CRITICISM

The Play in General

OF this play the fable is wild and pleasing. I know not how the ladies will approve the facility with which both Rosalind and Celia give up their hearts. To Celia much may be forgiven for the heroism of her friendship. The character of Jaques is natural and well-preserved. The comic dialogue is very sprightly, with less mixture of low buffoonery than in some other plays; and the graver part is elegant and harmonious. By hastening to the end of this work, Shakespeare suppressed the dialogue between the usurper and the hermit, and lost an opportunity of exhibiting a moral lesson in which he might have found matter worthy of his highest powers.

DR. JOHNSON, edition of Shakespeare (1765).

Shakespear has here converted the forest of Arden into another Arcadia, where they 'fleet the time carelessly, as they did in the golden world'. It is the most ideal of any of this author's plays. It is a pastoral drama, in which the interest arises more out of the sentiments and characters than out of the actions or situations. It is not what is done, but what is said, that claims our attention. Nursed in solitude, 'under the shade of melancholy boughs', the imagination grows soft and delicate, and the wit runs riot in idleness, like a spoiled child, that is never sent to school. Caprice and fancy reign and revel here, and stern necessity is banished to the court. The mild sentiments of humanity are strengthened with thought and leisure; the echo of the cares and noise of the world strikes upon the ear of those 'who have felt them knowingly', softened by time and distance. 'They hear the tumult, and are still.' The very air of the place seems to breathe a spirit of philosophical poetry: to stir the thoughts, to touch the heart with pity, as the drowsy forest rustles to the sighing gale. Never was there such beautiful moralising, equally free from pedantry or petulance.

> And this their life, exempt from public haunts,
> Finds tongues in trees, books in the running brooks,
> Sermons in stones, and good in everything.

Jaques is the only purely contemplative character in Shake-spear. He thinks, and does nothing. His whole occupation is to amuse his mind, and he is totally regardless of his body and his fortunes. He is the prince of philosophical idlers; his only passion is thought; he sets no value upon anything but as it serves as food for reflection. He can 'suck melancholy out of a song, as a weasel sucks eggs'; the motley fool, 'who morals on the time', is the greatest prize he meets with in the forest. He resents Orlando's passion for Rosalind as some disparagement of his own passion for abstract truth; and leaves the Duke, as soon as he is restored to his sovereignty, to seek his brother out who has quitted it, and turned hermit.

—'Out of these convertites
There is much matter to be heard and learnt.'

Within the sequestered and romantic glades of the forest of Arden, they find leisure to be good and wise, or to play the fool and fall in love. Rosalind's character is made up of sportive gaiety and natural tenderness: her tongue runs the faster to conceal the pressure at her heart. She talks herself out of breath, only to get deeper in love. The coquetry with which she plays with her lover in the double character which she has to support is managed with the nicest address. How full of voluble, laughing grace is all her conversation with Orlando:

—'In heedless mazes running
With wanton haste and giddy cunning.'

How full of real fondness and pretended cruelty is her answer to him when he promises to love her 'For ever and a day'!

'Say a day without the ever: no, no, Orlando, men are April when they woo, December when they wed: maids are May when they are maids, but the sky changes when they are wives: I will be more jealous of thee than a Barbary cock-pigeon over his hen; more clamorous than a parrot against rain; more new-fangled than an ape; more giddy in my desires than a monkey; I will weep for nothing like Diana in the fountain, and I will do that when you are disposed to be merry I will laugh like a hyen, and that when you are inclined to sleep.

Orlando. But will my Rosalind do so?

Rosalind. By my life she will do as I do.

found his characteristic formula; and we have nothing to do but to listen to the bugles blown as he hunts the quarry of his theme through the intricate glades and tangles of his bosky imagination. *As You Like It* is romance incarnate. All the wonderful elements of the secular tradition are gathered together there in its light-hearted compass. There is the romance of friendship in Rosalind and Celia, 'like Juno's swans, still coupled and inseparable'; the romance of Adam's loyalty, 'the constant service of the antique world'; the romance of love at first sight, acknowledged in words by the smitten Phebe's quotation of dead Marlowe's saw, and acknowledged as the mainspring of the whole plot when young Orlando wrestled and overthrew more than his enemies, and witty Rosalind, for all her cousin's warning, fell deeper in love than with safety of a pure blush she might in honour come off again. Then you have Orlando as the typical lover of romance, the love-shaked sonnetteer, hanging his odes upon hawthorns and his elegies upon brambles, and abusing the young plants with carving 'Rosalind' upon their barks. You have the conventional issues of romance in the wind-up of the story. . . . Above all, you have the romantic spirit of adventure with which the play is filled; and never more high-spirited and picturesque company of knight-errant and squire and dwarf set out on their enterprise in *Palmerin of England* and *Amadis of Gaul*, than this of Rosalind with curtle-axe upon her thigh, and Celia smirched with umber, and the roynish clown. *As You Like It* is one of the plays, so numerous above all at the midmost stage of Shakespeare's development, which are dominated by their women; and if one polled the company of readers for their choice of a heroine . . . it can hardly be doubted that the majority of suffrages would be Rosalind's. Witty and brave, audacious and tender, with a grace that her doublet and hose cannot pervert, and a womanhood that they cannot conceal, it is indeed she that gives the piece its special human charm, its note of sane and joyous vitality.

And yet, splendid as is Rosalind's, there is an even greater part in *As You Like It*. And that is the part of the Forest of Arden. We are always conscious of the forest in *As You Like It*. It is something more than a mere scenic background;

a spiritual force, bringing medicine to the hurt souls of men.
The banished duke has the sentiment of it—

> Hath not old custom made this life more sweet
> Than that of painted pomp? Are not these woods
> More free from peril than the envious court?

Thus *As You Like It* does for the Elizabethan drama what the
long string of pastoral poets, Spenser and Sidney, Lodge and
Greene, Drayton and Browne, and the rest, had already done,
or were still to do, for Elizabethan lyric. The temper of it is
not strictly the temper of the actual country-dweller as that
has filled our later literature for the last century. It is rather
the temper of urban disillusion, the instinctive craving of the
man who has been long in cities pent for green fields and quiet
nights. The pastoral impulse of the end of the sixteenth
century in England means that at the end of the sixteenth century Englishmen were learning to feel the oppression of cities.
And we know that, during the later years of Elizabeth and
the early years of James, statesmen were beginning to be pre-
occupied with the growth of London; that the builders were
pushing out along Holborn and the Strand; that the fields were
receding farther and farther into the distance; and that the
problems of overcrowding were becoming known. The monstrous nightmare of the modern city had not yet made its
appearance; but there was already reason enough, especially
in days when court intrigue was merciless and none too
savoury, for the finer souls to dream their dreams of Arcady
or of Arden.

And if Shakespeare dreamed, one is tempted to ask whether
he dreamed for others only, or for himself as well. One likes
to think that Shakespeare never became at heart a Londoner.
But all that is certain is that he never wholly cut himself
adrift from Stratford interests, since two or three years before
he wrote *As You Like It* he had already bought the fine
house there in which he was to end his days; and that in *As
You Like It* itself there breathes more of the country than in
any other play between *A Midsummer Night's Dream* and the
group which immediately preceded his retirement.

The fact that its theme is inspired by the reaction against

urban life naturally makes *As You Like It* a comedy as well as a romance. Its criticism is not only implied but direct. Consider the proceedings of Touchstone. Touchstone has been a courtier. . . . He gives himself airs accordingly; but, when he finds himself among the shepherds and shepherdesses, like the most capricious poet, honest Ovid, among the Goths, he certainly does not commend the court by the good sense or the decency of his love-making. He behaves, indeed, much like 'Arry in Epping. It is, however, to Jaques, rather than to Touchstone, that the function of voicing the satire of the play upon contemporary civilization chiefly belongs. Jaques is the professional cynic, always ready to rail against the first-born of Egypt and to pierce with his invective the body of the country, city, court. . . . Shakespeare's judgment of life is, indeed, too sane to let him even maintain the pretence that the perfection which is lacking at court will be found in the forest. Herein is the significance of the episode of the shepherdess Phebe, for Phebe is as vain and disdainful and wanton, and as remorseless in the prosecution of her selfish intrigues, as the finest lady of them all. She, no less than Oliver and Frederick, must learn her lesson.

And so we come to the point that the satire of the play is, after all, as much against as for the romantic ideals that the play sets out to expound; which is as much as to say, that the satire is converted into essential humour. . . . Once more an investigation of Touchstone is illuminating as to the intention of the dramatist. . . . It has often been observed that the fools of Shakespeare's plays have a sort of choric function. They are commentators rather than actors, and if you read them aright, you may catch in their fantastic utterance some reflection of the maker's own judgment upon his puppets. Herein Shakespeare is but true to an historic model. In mediaeval courts, where, as in all courts, the serious man must needs dissemble, it was always the privilege of those that wore the motley to speak a shrewd word in jest, to use their folly like a stalking-horse and under the presentation of that to shoot their wit. Touchstone, however, must, I think, be regarded as something of a variation upon the type. He embodies Shakespeare's comment upon romance, but it is

rather by what he is, than by anything that he consciously
says. For how can romance more readily be made ridiculous
than by the disconcerting contact of the natural gross man,
who blurts out in every crisis precisely those undesirable facts
which it is the whole object of romance to refine away? Adventure brings us to Arden, and it is left for the fool to realize
that when he was at home he was in a better place; nor can the
literary graces of love at first sight hold their own against
Touchstone's ready offer to 'rime you so, eight years together,
dinners and suppers and sleeping hours excepted.' It is doubt-
less only an accident of chronology, that Touchstone performs
exactly the same office of disillusion to the knight-errantry of
Rosalind and Orlando, as is performed by Sancho Panza to
that of the almost precisely contemporary Don Quixote de la
Mancha.

From E. K. CHAMBERS, *Shakespeare: A Survey* (1925).

The Love-Theme in the Play

IN this play love lives in many forms: in Orlando and Rosalind, Celia and Oliver, Silvius and Phoebe, Touchstone and
Audrey. We see also other forms of love: the love of the two
girls for one another, of Adam for his master and his master
for him, of Touchstone for Celia and Rosalind.

In this play also the lovers love one another at first sight.

> Dead shepherd, now I find thy saw of might:
> Who ever lov'd that lov'd not at first sight?

is the cry of Phoebe when she sees Rosalind, and thinks she is
a man. Rosalind is smitten the moment she sees Orlando,
Orlando when he sees Rosalind. When Oliver and Celia meet,
they 'no sooner saw one another but they loved.' . . .

The love-play of Orlando and Rosalind . . . is one of the
gayest things in Shakespeare. It is the natural bubbling up of
the fountain of happy youth into gracious gaiety of temper,
into self-delighting joy. We who listen, cannot enjoy the
humour of the situation when, dressed as a gallant hunter,
Rosalind meets Orlando, half as much as she enjoys it herself.
She plays with it as a kitten with a ball. Her love develops,

does not check or dim, her humour. As to her natural intellect, it is the same with that. Love has not impaired it. It is as swift and various as summer lightning; and though it flashes here and there and everywhere, it always strikes the point at issue. It sees into the centre of all masked conventions. It understands Jaques in a moment, though he is a man of the world and she a girl; and lays him bare to himself. Yet all the time this clear-eyed intellect is working on life, she is so deep in love that it cannot be sounded. In her, emotion and intellect are equal powers. . . .

Orlando's love is of the same quality, full of gaiety, even though—for he cannot find Rosalind—it be dashed with a shade of natural melancholy: amusing itself with delightful verses hung on happy trees, ready to play with the pretty youth he is pleased to call his Rosalind; witty enough to make the talk lively, not witty enough to displease the girl who would not wish him to be brilliant when he thought he was away from her; of a grave intelligence also when he chooses; able, like Rosalind, to overcome Jaques with his own weapons.

The love of Celia and Oliver is of a different kind . . . and I think Shakespeare has been betrayed into inventing something which is not quite in nature by his desire to wind up his play by such a reconciliation of Oliver and Orlando as will make everything comfortable for Rosalind and Orlando in the future.

The love of Silvius and Phoebe is the conventional love of the Elizabethan Pastoral; and it may be, in this love-drama, a satire on that academic, literary love. But he touches the love of Silvius with reality. Its expression goes far beyond the conventional phrasing of the Pastoral. It seems a pity that Silvius is almost too great a fool for any woman to care for. But he is in earnest, and Rosalind sees that he is; and while she strives to lash him into rebellion against Phoebe, she also takes some pains to get his sweetheart for him in the end. She does not pity him, for his want of manliness deserves no pity; but she uses Phoebe's love for her (as a man) to soften her heart, to make her understand what Silvius has suffered; and, in that new temper, Phoebe takes Silvius because he has been faithful. The conventional love is led into the natural; and the way it is managed is as pretty a piece of work as is to be found in Shakespeare.

STOPFORD BROOKE, On Ten Plays of Shakespeare (1905).

The Character of Rosalind

ROSALIND and Orlando do not overtop or overweight the play. Shakespeare's dramatic genius has now matured. The too great dominance of the leading characters—that common mistake of dramatists into which Shakespeare seems to have fallen in *Richard II* and *III*—is now quite absent from his work. And yet, Rosalind does not lose her supremacy. She is still first, but first, not because she is isolated from the other characters, but because she adds life to all that is living in them. She does not put out their light, but kindles it into a brighter flame of character. They burn all the brighter for her influence. A touch from her makes them reveal themselves.

In the first act, Rosalind, Celia, and Orlando are not the gay persons they are afterwards; and no wonder, their circumstances are disagreeable. The suppressed spirit of their youth is longing for freedom. Rosalind, having this longing—and her father's exile and her uncle's jealousy of her intensify it—is sad enough. Yet in her light liftings out of sadness we hear the far-off music of what is coming, the prelude to the happiness of her forest love-adventure. In her sadness also, and because of it, a part of her character is developed by Shakespeare which we might not have divined from the following acts. We see the seriousness, the deep feeling, the solid sense, which lie beneath her youthful brightness. She cannot 'forget her banished father', cannot take part in any 'extraordinary pleasure.' She has now the reticent courtesy, the grave dignity and courage of a great lady. . . .

But she does not allow her common-sense or her sadness in this first act to interfere with the affairs of love. There she lets Nature have her way, and slips into her love with delight; . . . And with the joy comes, of course, the sweet and tender melancholy of love which knows not yet that it is returned, but is all but sure it is; and which in puffs of alternate painful pleasure and pleasurable pain makes its own drama in the heart.

With this grave, gay girlhood, with this beauty, she has also intellect and its charm. Celia has quite enough, but Rosalind overbrims with it. It is a natural growth in her, and comes of her divine vitality. It illuminates her argument with Celia on the gifts of Nature and Fortune, but there Celia is as quick-minded as she. It is only when she gets to the forest, and is warmed by meeting Orlando, that it develops into sparkle of wit, into power, insight, and good sense. Corin is the honest labourer, old, tired, and practical, but who has had his day of love in youth and remembers it. This hallows his age, and makes it sweet with thought, for Shakespeare was too kindly to leave the old unblessed. And Rosalind likes the old labour-er, and he understands Rosalind. When he talks with her, he rises above his natural level of thought, so greatly does her presence heighten and kindle whomsoever she touches. It is the Corin whom love plagued of old, who makes this speech when he calls Rosalind to see Silvius and Phoebe meeting—

> If you will see a pageant truly play'd,
> Between the pale complexion of true love
> And the red glow of scorn and proud disdain,
> Go hence a little, and I shall conduct you,
> If you will mark it.

That is the kindling of Rosalind. Corin is breathing the poetic air of his youth. The years of long labour are forgotten in her presence.

STOPFORD BROOKE, *On Ten Plays of Shakespeare* (1905).

The Character of Jaques

THE play has been represented . . . as an early attempt made by the poet to control the dark spirit of melancholy in himself 'by thinking it away.' The characters of the banished Duke, of Orlando, of Rosalind are described as three gradations of cheerfulness in adversity, with Jaques placed over against them in designed contrast. But no real adversity has come to any one of them. Shakspere, when he put into the Duke's mouth the words, 'Sweet are the uses of adversity,' knew something of deeper affliction than a life in the golden leisure of Arden. Of real melancholy there is none in the play; for the melancholy of Jaques is not grave and earnest, but sentimental,

a self-indulgent humour, a petted foible of character, melancholy prepense and cultivated; 'it is a melancholy of mine
own, compounded of many simples, extracted from many
objects; and indeed the sundry contemplation of my travels,
in which my often rumination wraps me in a most humorous
sadness.' The Duke declares that Jaques has been 'a libertine, as sensual as the brutish sting itself;' but the Duke is
unable to understand such a character as that of Jaques.
Jaques has been no more than a curious experimenter in
libertinism, for the sake of adding an experience of madness and
folly to the store of various superficial experiences which constitute his unpractical foolery of wisdom. The haunts of sin
have been visited as a part of his travel. By and by he will go
to the usurping Duke who has put on a religious life, because

> Out of these convertites
> There is much matter to be heard and learned.

Jaques knows no bonds that unite him to any living thing.
He lives upon novel, curious, and delicate sensations. . . . 'A
fool! a fool! I met a fool i' the forest!'—and in the delight of
coming upon this exquisite surprise, Jaques laughs like chanticleer,

> Sans intermission
> An hour by his dial.

His whole life is unsubstantial and unreal; a curiosity of dainty
mockery. To him 'all the world's a stage, and all the men and
women merely players;' to him sentiment stands in place of
passion; an aesthetic, amateurish experience of various modes
of life stands in place of practical wisdom; and words, in place
of deeds. . . . Jaques in his own way supposes that he can
dispense with realities. The world, not as it is, but as it mirrors
itself in his own mind, which gives to each object a humorous
distortion, this is what alone interests Jaques. Shakspere would
say to us, 'This egoistic, contemplative, unreal manner of treating life is only a delicate kind of foolery. Real knowledge
of life can never be acquired by the curious seeker for experiences.' But this Shakspere says in his nonhortatory, un-
dogmatic way.

EDWARD DOWDEN, *Shakspere: his Mind and Art* (1901).

The play treats of the gifts of Nature and the ways of Fortune. Orlando, given little, is brought to much. Rosalind and Celia, born to much, are brought to little. The Duke, born to all things, is brought to nothing. The usurping Duke, born to nothing, climbs to much, desires all, and at last renounces all. Oliver, born to much, aims at a little more, loses all, and at last regains all. Touchstone, the worldly wise, marries a fool. Audrey, born a clown, marries a courtier. Phebe, scorning a man, falls in love with a woman.

Jaques, the only wise one, is the only one not moved by Fortune. Life does not interest him; his interest is in his thoughts about life. His vision of life feasts him whatever life does . . . The wisest of Shakespeare's characters are often detached from the action of the play in which they appear. Jaques holds aloof from the action of this play, though he is perhaps the best-known character in the cast. His thought is the thought of all wise men, that wisdom, being always a little beyond the world, has no worldly machinery by which it can express itself. In this world the place of chorus, interpreter or commentator is not given to the wise man, but to the fool who has degraded the office to a profession. Jaques, the wise man, finds the place occupied by one whose comment is platitude. Wisdom has no place in the social scheme. The fool, he finds, has both office and uniform.

Seeing this, Jaques wishes, as all wise men wish, not to be counted wise but to have as great liberty as the fool to express his thought—

> 'weed your better judgments
> Of all opinion that grows rank in them
> That I am wise. I must have liberty
> Withal, as large a charter as the wind,
> To blow on whom I please; for so fools have.

> . . . give me leave
> To speak my mind, and I will through and through
> Cleanse the foul body of the infected world,
> If they will patiently receive my medicine.'

He is answered that, having learned of the world's evil by libidinous living, he can only do evil by exposing his knowledge. He replies, finely expressing Shakespeare's invariable

artistic practice, that his aim will be at sin, not at particular
sinners.

In the middle of his speech Orlando enters, raging for food.
It is interesting to see how closely Shakespeare follows Jaques'
mind in the presence of the fierce animal want of hunger. He is
too much interested to be of help. The Duke ministers to Orlando. Jaques wants to know 'of what kind this cock should
come of.' He speaks banteringly, the Duke speaks kindly.
The impression given is that Jaques is heartless. The Duke's
thought is 'here is one even more wretched than ourselves.'
Jaques' thought, always more for humanity than for the individual, is a profound vision of the world.

The play is a little picture of the world. The contemplative
man who is not of the world, is yet a part of the picture. We
are shown a company of delightful people, just escaped from
disaster, smilingly taking the biggest of hazards. The wise man,
dismissing them to their fates with all the authority of wisdom,
gives up his share in the game to listen to a man who has given
up his share of the world. Renunciation of the world is attractive to all upon whom the world presses very heavily, or very
lightly.

Rosalind and Phebe are of the two kinds of woman who come
much into Shakespeare's early and middle plays. Rosalind,
like Portia, is a golden woman, a daughter of the sun, smiling-
natured, but limited. Phebe, like Rosaline, is black-haired,
black-eyed, black-eyebrowed, with the dead-white face that so
often goes with cruelty.   JOHN MASEFIELD, *Shakespeare* (1911).

The Character of Touchstone

... Touchstone is no ordinary comic figure ; he is the representative, and easily the best representative (Falstaff stands by
himself), of a special class of comic figures. Unlike most other
humorous characters, he has no unconscious absurdities, and
that is why he cannot be counted among those who wear the
fine flower of the ridiculous ; he is not laughable in himself, he
is only droll by vocation. Although he is a Clown, a Fool, he is
obviously a superior member of his order ; he is no common
buffoon making the most of some natural deformity and finding

his fun in bladder play and monkey tricks, but the first of Shakespeare's great Fools, a professional wit and humorist. . . . Nor must it be forgotten that the fashion in wit changes, and that the poor nonsense that Touchstone occasionally achieves once passed for wit. When Elizabeth's dramatists and poets were all scribbling and the playhouses were packed, language was like a new glittering toy that had only to be tossed rapidly from speaker to speaker to set the house in a roar. The verbal battledore and shuttlecock played by Rosalind, Celia, and Touchstone in the first act of *As You Like It* may seem a poor game to us now, but there was a time, before a ball had bounced at Lord's or Wimbledon, when it was as enthralling as good cricket or tennis. And even in these scenes there is a taste of the 'dull fool's' real quality. The Duke puts the matter in a nutshell when he says of Touchstone: 'He uses his folly as a stalking-horse, and under the presentation of that, he shoots his wit.'

The two persons who know him best, and who are responsible for his being in the forest at all, Rosalind and Celia, rather miss his real character: they see the Fool but are blind to the comic philosopher. To them he is 'the clownish fool.' It is true that Rosalind has her suspicions. . . . But if Rosalind and Celia hardly testify to Touchstone's quality as a humorist, they do show us, in one flash, something of his quality as a man. They pay him a magnificent compliment, for they single him out to be their companion in their flight to Arden. . . . This shows us a new Touchstone. . . . When the three of them stagger into the forest, Rosalind crying, 'Well, this is the Forest of Arden,' and Touchstone replying, 'Ay, now am I in Arden; the more fool I; when I was at home, I was in a better place; but travellers must be content'; he speaks only the bare truth. He has flung away safety and comfort and applause for a lady's whim, and has thereby betrayed his genial cynicism.

Romance, however, having enticed him into her own green Arcadia, has to be content with that and nothing more, for once there, Touchstone returns to his ancient loyalties and promptly goes about his own business of parody and mockery, of clowning illuminated by criticism.

And as it is both his business and his pleasure to mock the fashion of the hour, he does not fail to play the pastoral lover himself. If Orlando must have his Rosalind, Oliver his Celia, Silvius his Phebe, so Touchstone must have his Audrey. . . . There is no conventional shepherdess, no lovely pink-and-white and entirely unreal Phebe, for him; he stays outside the pastoral and remains in this world, and so has to be content with an Audrey, that is, with the kind of damsel really to be found in the countryside, neither superlatively beautiful nor intelligent, but a great gawky country lass.

He can indite verses as good as, if not better than, those of Orlando, and he certainly has more wit, but Audrey, good soul, cannot even pretend to poetry, and has, indeed, a most disarming knowledge of her own limitations, even confessing to a want of beauty, which may be joined in time, in Touch-stone's opinion, by other defects, notably sluttishness. None of this, however, disturbs the ironist in motley for an instant: he revels in the incongruity of it all. The relation between Touchstone and his stolid mistress is really nothing but the reverse side, the unpoetical, comic, gross side, of the relation between Orlando and Rosalind, all ardour and bloom and young laughter, beyond the reach of disillusion.

That Touchstone's courtship of Audrey, as Hazlitt remarks, 'throws a degree of ridicule on the state of wedlock itself,' must be admitted, but . . . there is, in the last resort, more to be said about his queer courtship than this, more, indeed, than has apparently been said anywhere. That he is not seriously in love is obvious enough, but this is probably only because he cannot be entirely serious about anything. Even his surprisingly romantic devotion to his young mistress Celia probably has a comical air: we have not heard him on the subject. Yet it is quite possible that a lapse of time that would find Oliver deserting Celia and taking to the forest again to haunt the neighbourhood of Phebe, now the bored wife of Silvius, would also find Touchstone and Audrey still jogging along together, the gentleman still making mysterious jests and criticisms, and the lady fixing her stolid gaze upon the solid fruits of his jesting and not troubling her head about his whims and fancies. And consider, before we leave him,

Touchstone's introduction of his Audrey to the Duke: 'A poor virgin, sir, an ill-favour'd thing, sir, but mine own.' This, it will be said, is not the speech of a man in love; nor is it, but it might very well be the speech of a humorist, a dry, sceptical humorist, who is as near to being in love as he is likely to be. . . . This world being what it is—and how well Motley knows the world—it describes with more accuracy than all the honeyed, golden speeches of our Romeos and Antonies the actual feelings that men and women, not poets and born lovers, ever ready to shower glittering words upon any newly found deity, but workaday men and women, have for one another; and as your mood runs, you may throw the emphasis upon 'the ill-favour'd thing' and laugh away the follies of youth; or, more justly, you may wait for the end of the phrase and see the significance, the odd pathos that somehow finds its way into all human relations, of the last three words, 'but mine own,' and so fall to wondering rather than laughing or perhaps to doing both at once.

J. B. PRIESTLEY, *The English Comic Characters* (1925).

THE LIFE OF WILLIAM SHAKESPEARE

(condensed from Sir Edmund Chambers's *William Shakespeare*)

WILLIAM SHAKESPEARE was born of middle-class parents at Stratford-on-Avon, a provincial market town of some importance, at an uncertain date between April 24, 1563, and April 23, 1564. His parents were natives of Warwickshire. His father, John Shakespeare, whose principal business was that of glover, rose high in civic life, becoming alderman in 1565 and bailiff in 1568, but later fell on evil days. His mother was Mary Arden. Shakespeare was educated at King Edward VI's Grammar School, Stratford, where he must have learnt a fair amount of Latin, if little or no Greek. He married in 1582 Anne Hathaway, and his first child, Susanna, was baptized in May 1583, to be followed in February 1585 by twins, Hamnet and Judith. Susanna's daughter, Elizabeth (died 1670), was the poet's last direct descendant.

We have no certain information as to Shakespeare's life between 1584 and 1592. There is an early tradition that he stole deer from Sir T. Lucy of Charlecote. We know Shakespeare was in London by 1592 but not when he went there. During these years Shakespeare must have acquired the varied knowledge and experience of life shown in his plays.

The mention of Shakespeare in a death-bed letter of the playwright Green in September 1592 shows that as a writer for the stage Shakespeare was just becoming a serious rival to the university wits—Marlowe, Peele, Nashe, and Lodge. The years when the theatres were closed on account of plague gave time for the poems, *Venus and Adonis* (1593) and *Lucrece* (1594), both dedicated to the Earl of Southampton. By March 1595 Shakespeare was a shareholder in the acting company of the Lord Chamberlain's men who divided with the Admiral's men the command of the London stage from about 1594 to 1603. For this company, which later became the King's men, Shakespeare seems to have written during the rest of his career. After 1599 most of his plays were performed at the Globe Theatre.

Shakespeare probably wrote his *Sonnets* between 1595 and 1600, but they were not printed till 1609.

In 1596 Shakespeare obtained a grant of arms; in 1597 he bought New Place, a substantial house and garden at Stratford, but he is still found living in London in 1597, 1599, and 1604. Shakespeare occasionally appeared as an actor himself, chiefly before 1598.

About 1610 Shakespeare retired to Stratford, and he wrote no more after 1613. He took no part in civic life, and died on April 23, 1616. There is no reason to reject the report that he died of fever contracted from drinking too hard at a merry meeting with Drayton and Ben Jonson.

TABLE OF APPROXIMATE DATES OF SHAKESPEARE'S PLAYS

1590–1.

    2 Henry VI.
    3 Henry VI.

1591–2.

    1 Henry VI.

1592–3.

    Richard III.
    Comedy of Errors.

1593–4.

    Titus Andronicus.
    Taming of the Shrew.

1594–5.

    Two Gentlemen of Verona.
    Love's Labour's Lost.
    Romeo and Juliet.

1595–6.

    Richard II.
    Midsummer-Night's Dream.

1596–7.

    King John.
    Merchant of Venice.

1597–8.

    1 Henry IV.
    2 Henry IV.

1598–9.

    Much Ado About Nothing.
    Henry V.

1599–1600.

    Julius Caesar.
    As You Like It.
    Twelfth Night.

1600–1.
  Hamlet.
  Merry Wives of Windsor.

1601–2.
  Troilus and Cressida.

1602–3.
  All's Well That Ends Well.

1603–4.

———

1604–5.
  Measure for Measure.
  Othello.

1605–6.
  King Lear.
  Macbeth.

1606–7.
  Antony and Cleopatra.

1607–8.
  Coriolanus.
  Timon of Athens.

1608–9.
  Pericles.

1609–10.
  Cymbeline.

1610–11.
  Winter's Tale.

1611–12.
  Tempest.

1612–13.
  Henry VIII.
  Two Noble Kinsmen.

APPENDIX II

A NOTE ON SHAKESPEARE'S LANGUAGE

By C. T. ONIONS

VOCABULARY. As the *Oxford Shakespeare Glossary* shows, there are some ten thousand words in the whole of the works attributed to Shakespeare which require explanation for the general reader, either because they are no longer in ordinary use or because they are used by him in some way that is not now familiar. Among the former are such words as *ballow* cudgel, *phill-horse* shaft-horse, and *neaf* fist, which are now only provincial, and such others as *benison* blessing, *foison* abundance, *mow* grimace, *parlous* dangerous, *puissant* powerful, *teen* grief, which may be found still in literary diction, as well as a considerable number that have been used, so far as we know, by Shakespeare alone. With such as these we become acquainted by reference to glossaries and notes. But it is possible to continue to read Shakespeare without properly understanding him because we are unaware of, and sometimes do not even suspect, differences in the meaning of words that are in general use to-day. The following selection of such words will serve to indicate the nature of the differences that may be looked for:

allow approve
argument proof, subject of discourse
brave fine, splendid
churchman clergyman
close secret
complexion habit or constitution of body or mind, look, aspect, appearance
conceit idea, thought, invention
condition covenant, rank, character
difference disagreement, dispute
evil disease
fashion sort
favour appearance, face
feature bodily form
gear affair, business
grudge complain
hint opportunity
hope expect, suppose
infer allege
instance cause, evidence; proof
level aim
lewd bad, vile

liberal unrestrained, licentious
mere absolute, downright
merely entirely
miss do without
note sign, stigma, information
obsequious dutiful
owe own
painful laborious
passion painful disease, strong emotion
peevish silly, perverse
present immediate
presently at once
prevent anticipate
quality rank, profession
rate estimation
respect consideration
sad grave, serious
shrewd mischievous, bad
sort rank, class, way, manner
still always, continually
stomach inclination, angry or proud temper
sudden swift, violent
tall fine, valiant
type mark, badge
very true, complete

Among words having a very wide range of meaning the following may be noted:

humour (1) moisture, (2) any of the four fluids of the human body recognized by the old physiologists, (3) temperament, (4) mood, temper, fancy, caprice, inclination;

nice (1) delicate, (2) shy, coy, (3) fastidious, (4) subtle, minute, (5) trivial, (6) critical, precarious, (7) exact, precise;

quaint (1) skilled, clever, (2) pretty, dainty, (3) handsome, elegant, (4) carefully elaborated;

sensible (1) sensitive, (2) of the senses, (3) capable of emotion, (4) rational, (5) tangible, substantial, (6) full of good sense;

wit (1) mental powers, mind, faculty of perception, as in *the five wits*, (2) inventive power, (3) understanding, intelligence, (4) wisdom, good sense, as in *brevity is the soul of wit*, (5) lively fancy producing brilliant talk.

A second adjective **dear** grievous, severe, dire (distinct from *dear* beloved, precious) is seen in *my dear offence, thy dear exile*.

Many adjectives and participial words show the application of a suffix with a force different from that which is now usual:

deceivable deceitful	**questionable** inviting question
tuneable tuneful	**careless** uncared for
unmeritable undeserving	**unexpressive** inexpressible
cureless incurable	**plausive** plausible
grac'd gracious	**unavoided** inevitable
guiled treacherous	**beholding** obliged, beholden
disdain'd disdainful	**timeless** untimely, premature

Note also the double meaning, active and passive, of **artificial** (1) constructive, creative, (2) produced by art.

Shakespeare uses a multitude of technical terms of the arts and sciences; these are treated in their historical setting in *Shakespeare's England* (O.U.P.); note especially the glossary of musical terms in vol. ii, pp. 32 ff. Some general aspects of the vocabulary are dealt with in G. S. Gordon's *Shakespeare's English*, Society for Pure English, Tract xxix (O.U.P.).

PRONUNCIATION. In order to understand the scansion of the verse it is necessary to bear in mind certain features of the pronunciation of the time. Many words of French or Latin origin had been variously stressed from early times, and deviation from present usage is to be seen, for example, in Shakespeare's *adver'tizèd, aspect', canon'izèd, chas'tise, compact'* (noun), *exile', instinct'* (noun), *obdu'rate, reven'ue, sepul'chre, solem'nizèd, triumph'ing*. The stressing of certain adjectives and participles of two syllables is subject to the rule that immediately before nouns of one syllable, and before other nouns stressed on the first syllable, they themselves are stressed on the first syllable, but in other positions on the second; thus: *all' the com'plete ar'mour, ev'ery way' complete'; the en'tire sum', your' entire' affec'tion; the crown' so foul' misplaced', the mis'placed John'*.

In words in *-ian, -ience, -ient, -ion*, these endings may count as two syllables; thus, *Christian, patient* may be 3 syllables, *condition, impatience* 4, *lamentation* 5. Similarly *marriage* and *soldier* may be three syllables. There is variation in such words as *fire, hour, power, prayer*, which may count as either one or two syllables. *Either* and *neither* may be slurred into one syllable, and *whether* is often so reduced, the form *where* frequently occurring in the old editions, continuing what was a regular early English variant form. *Hither, thither, whither,* and *having, evil, devil* are treated in the same way. *Statue* occurs in several passages in the old editions where three syllables are required; many modern editions substitute *statua,* which was a common Tudor and Stuart form.

NOUNS. The genitive singular ending *s* may be replaced by *his*, as *the Count* his *galleys, Mars* his *armour*. The inflexion is dropped before *sake*, e.g. *for justice sake, for heaven sake*. Proper names often occur without inflexion, where the genitive might be expected, or *of*: e.g. *Venice gold, Rome gates, Tiber banks*. One of the adverbial uses of the genitive is preserved in *come your ways*. Notable examples of the *n*-plural are *shoon* for *shoes*, and *eyne* (eyes), which are used chiefly for rhyme. *Aches* is of two syllables, since the noun *ache* was pronounced *aitch*, as distinct from the verb, which was regularly spelt *ake* in the old editions. Names of measures and periods of time are often un-inflected, as *twelve year, a thousand pound*: cf. *sennight* (= seven nights) week.

ADJECTIVES. Adjectives are converted into nouns with greater freedom than at present: *fair* is used for beauty as well as for lady, *the general* for the public, the multitude, *the subject* for the people of a state. Note the phrases: *in few* in few words, in short; *by small and small* little by little; *the most* (= majority) *of men*. *Enow* represents the old plural of *enough*, and is so used, always following its noun or pronoun. *Mo, moe* (= more) is also plural: it represents an old comparative adverb, which was used at first with a genitive, but became in time an adjective like *more*. The plural of *other* is either *others* or *other* (e.g. *and then come in the other*).

Peculiarities in the comparison of adjectives are: the use of the suffixes where we prefer *more* and *most*, as *certainer, per-fecter, violentest*; the addition of *-er* to a comparative, as *worser*; the use of *more* and *most* with comparatives and superlatives, as *more better, most best, most dearest, more worthier, most worst, most unkindest*. Note the old comparative *near*, as in *ne'er the near*. An absolute superlative may be strengthened by prefixing *one*, e.g. *one the truest-mannered*.

PRONOUNS. The distinction between the familiar or con-temptuous *thou* (*thee, thy*) and the respectful *ye* (*you, your*) is in general preserved. The old weak form *a* of *he* occurs in *There was a gaming*. The commonest genitive of *it* is *his*; the present-day *its* and the obsolete *it* (as in *It had it head bit off by it young*) are about equally frequent in the old editions. Pronominal pos-sessive forms are sometimes used as adjectives, but only in company with other possessives, as in *his and* **mine** *lov'd darling*. Note the position of the possessive in *good* **my** *liege, sweet* **my** *coz*.

There is much irregularity in the use of the cases of pronouns. *Thee* is used for *thou*, as with intransitive imperatives, *look thee, stand thee close*; also in *I would not be thee*, and the like. We find also: *between you and* I; *Is she as tall as* me?; *Which, of* he *or Adrian . . . ?; Damn'd be* him *. . .* The functions of the original nominative *ye* and objective *you* are reversed in *I do beseech* ye, *if* you *bear me hard . . .; us* is usual for *we* in the interrogative *Shall's*. There is no consistency in the use of *who* and *whom*; a common confusion is illustrated in **whom** *they say is killed*.

The relative pronouns are not discriminated according to present practice, since *which* may refer to persons and *who* to things. *The which* is very frequent; it may be used adjectivally, as in *For the which blessing I am at him upon my knees*. The nominative relative (the subject of the clause) is often absent, as in *There be some sports are painful*. After a negative or an interrogative, *but* is frequently used as a relative = that . . . not; e.g. *No man* but *prophesied revenge for it; What canst thou say* but *will perplex them more?*

VERBS. Verbs show many old forms as well as a variety of conjugation which are no longer possible in ordinary language.

Early strong forms are retained in *holp, holp'st,* alongside *helped, helped'st; spake* and *spoke* are both in use; old strong forms are replaced by weak in *becomed, shaked;* the past tenses *drunk* and *sprung* are more frequent than *drank* and *sprang;* the clipped *broke, spoke* occur beside the fuller participial forms *broken, spoken; catched* and *caught* are both found; many past tense forms are used for the past participle, as *eat, holp, forsook, rode, shook, swam*. Remarkable instances of the great variety of usage may be seen in *struck, strucken, stricken,* for the past participle of *strike,* and in the conjugation *write,* past tense *writ,* occasionally *wrote,* past participle *written, writ,* less frequently *wrote*. Weak verbs of which the stem ends in *d* or *t* often have shortened past tenses and past participles, as *betid, heat, sweat, wed, wet*. Observe that *graft* and *hoist* are rather participles of the older verbs *graff* and *hoise* than of *graft* and *hoist*.

Present tense forms in *s* (including *is*) are not uncommonly used with plural subjects, especially where the verb precedes the subject; e.g. *What cares these roarers for the name of king?; There* is *no more such masters*.

There are many survivals of impersonal uses, some of them in disguise. The older forms of *I were better, Thou'rt best* were *Me were better* It would be better for me, *Thee were best* It would be best for thee; but in *You were better* the case of the pronoun became ambiguous, *you* was in time felt as a nominative, and other pronouns fell into line. The history of the development of *I am woe* (in which *woe* is felt as an adjective) from the original *Me is woe* is somewhat similar. In *Fair befall thee* the verb is impersonal and *fair* an adverb.

The uses of the subjunctive are many and various. An exceptional construction is seen in **Live** *thou* (= if thou live), *I live*. An old use of the past subjunctive is exemplified in *If you would put me to verses, Kate, why, you* **undid** (= would undo) *me*.

The infinitive of a verb of motion is often to be supplied in thought with an auxiliary verb; e.g. *I must to England;* **Shall** *we to this gear?*

ADVERBS. Adverbs, especially those of one syllable, may have the same form as their corresponding adjectives, as *dear, full, fair, near, true*; such words as *excellent, equal, instant, prodigal* are also used adverbially. When two adverbs are coupled together which would both normally have the suffix *-ly*, one of them may lack it, as in *sprightfully and bold, so lamely and unfashionable*. A rare formation is *chirurgeonly* like a surgeon. Comparative forms with the suffix are used more freely than at present; e.g. *earth*lier *happy, wise*lier.

The use of *but* in the sense of 'only' needs to be specially noticed: *but now* just now, only this moment; similarly *but while-ere* only a short time ago, *but late* only lately. It is coupled redundantly with *only* in *He only lived but till he was a man*.

Normally, *only* should stand immediately before the words it modifies; but it is often loosely placed, as in *He only loves the world for him* (i.e. only for him).

A negative adverb (or conjunction) may be used with another negative word, superfluously from our point of view (the use was originally emphatic): *You know my father hath no child but I,* **nor** *none is like to have*. The negative may even be tripled: *Love no man in good earnest;* **nor** *no further in sport* **neither**. In the following a redundant negative occurs in a dependent clause after a verb of negative meaning: *You may deny that you were* **not** *the cause*.

PREPOSITIONS. Prepositions have many uses that differ from their present ones; for example, *for, of,* and *to* have each some ten meanings that are not current now. *Of* and *with* are both used to express the agent, as in *seen of us, torn to pieces with a bear,* or the instrument, as in *provided of a torch-bearer, killed with a thunderstroke.* With abstract nouns, *of* forms equivalents of the corresponding adjectives; e.g. *of desperation* desperate, *of nature* natural. Both *for* and *to* may be used, though in different kinds of context, = in the character of, as: e.g. *turned out of all towns and cities* for *a dangerous thing; I have a king here* to *my flatterer.* A preposition is used freely at the end of the sentence or clause, e.g. *he I am before* = he in whose presence I am; sometimes it is redundant, as in *the scene wherein we play* in; or again, it may be dropped, as in *I see thou lovest me not with the full weight that I love thee* (i.e. *with*).

At in *at door, at gate,* and the like, is descended from the earlier *atte* (two syllables), which is for *at the.*

CONJUNCTIONS. The following should be noted: *an* or *an if* if; *as* as if; *for* because; *but* if . . . not, unless; *nor* . . *nor* . . neither . . nor . ., *or* . . *or* . . either . . or . .; *or ere* before ever; *so* provided that; *that* (in much wider use than at present) for the reason that, because, in order that, so that; *whiles* while.

The full exposition of the language of Shakespeare requires a book to itself, and such will be found in E. A. Abbott's *Shakespearian Grammar* and W. Franz's *Shakespeare-Grammatik.* An illuminating sketch is Henry Bradley's essay 'Shakespeare's English' in *Shakespeare's England,* vol. ii, pp. 539–74. Selected points are treated with some fullness in *Nine Plays of Shakespeare* (O.U.P.), pp. xix–xxxvi.

APPENDIX III

A NOTE ON METRE

SHAKESPEARE'S plays are written in blank (i.e. unrhymed) verse with a varying proportion of prose and an occasional song in lyric metres in some plays, as in this one. As a rule, only the comic characters or those of lower rank speak prose, verse being almost invariable for more dignified speakers and purposes. But more than half of *As You Like It* is written in prose: all the comic scenes and passages, and most of those where Rosalind, Celia, and Orlando are the chief speakers. The usual division, however, is broadly observed, for the two Dukes invariably use verse, as do their followers in addressing them. Even the irrepressible Rosalind, who always uses free and flexible prose when she can, speaks in verse to the usurping Duke and her father. It is an interesting distinction that the conventional shepherd and shepherdess, Silvius and Phebe, also speak in verse—and Corin, except to Touchstone; but William and Audrey in prose. In the verse a good many rhyming couplets are to be found, which ring the close of a scene or episode, or have the effect of clinching a statement. Hymen talks in rhymed verse, in accordance with an established tradition of the masque; and in the songs and 'verses' scattered through the play the lyric forms are varied from the pretty pattern of Amiens' songs to Touchstone's doggerel, the alternate rhymes of 'Why should this a desert be?' to the 'false gallop' of the verses in which first Orlando and then Touchstone tries how many rhymes he can find to Rosa*lind*.

Blank verse had been in use on the Elizabethan stage for a generation, and about 1590 Christopher Marlowe had brought it to perfection in his 'mighty line'. Although all unrhymed verse might be called 'blank verse', the name is specially applied to the line consisting *normally* of ten syllables with five stresses or accents. It is common to use the terminology of classical verse, and, if we understand that a long syllable in Latin or Greek corresponds to an accented or 'more conspicuous' syllable in English, we may describe blank verse as five iambic feet (i.e. five feet each consisting of an iambus, scanning ∪ –). But whereas in classical verse quantity was rigid and the variations allowed from the pattern were strictly limited, in English verse very few lines conform absolutely to the pattern by having an equally strong accent on five of ten syllables. In Shakespeare not only is the accent either altogether absent, or reversed (– ∪ for ∪ –), in some feet, but often we have more, and occasionally fewer, than ten syllables in a line. A poet can make almost any departure from the norm, provided he does not destroy the sense of that pattern underlying his verse in the reader's mind. It is essential for all readers of Shake-

speare first to acquire a consciousness of the pattern, and for
this purpose they may scan lines by stressing the syllables that
should bear an accent, thus:

With e´yes | seve´re | and bea´rd | of fo´r|mal cu´t . . .

(II. vii. 155)

But very few of the thirty lines of this famous speech will be
found to conform to the pattern.

Some of the verse of *As You Like It* approximates to Shakespeare's earlier manner: the sense often ends with the line
and several lines in sequence keep the regular beat. When he
is merely getting through 'business', or his speaker is an
exalted person in whom, for the moment, he is not particularly
interested, Shakespeare often continues to write this stiffer
verse after his natural manner has changed. Passages such as
Jaques' speech are more characteristic of the blank verse of his
'middle period', in which the pauses, even more the stresses,
are very freely distributed, and the phrase-groups closely
approximate to the order of dramatic speech. It is worth
noting, too, that in *As You Like It* are to be found several
lines which look like, and may be, alexandrines (see III. v. 74;
IV. iii. 8; V. iv. 60–1); double endings are not unusual; and
weak endings occur in II. i. 60–1; IV. iii. 118–19. In reading
this kind of blank verse, therefore, the ear remains aware of
the underlying movement and the regular pattern, but in fact
it is the variety of the modulations that is most interesting and
audible.

(For a brief treatment of Shakespeare's variations such as
extra syllables, 'weak endings', &c., see Dowden's *Shakespeare
Primer*, pp. 39, &c., and for a more general view of the subject
E. Hamer's *The Metres of English Poetry*.)

APPENDIX IV

SUMMARY OF LODGE'S ROSALYNDE

A worthy knight, Sir John of Bordeaux, left three sons.
The second, Fernandyne, departed to follow his studies; and
the eldest, Saladyne, ignoring his father's injunction to care
for the youngest, Rosader, kept him in a dependent, servile

condition. Come to man's estate, Rosader rebelled against such treatment, till Saladyne saw a chance to get rid of him in a wrestling tournament, at which a noted champion was to stand against all comers. The rank and beauty of France were to be present, including the usurping king, Torismond, his daughter, Alinda, and her cousin Rosalynd, the daughter of Gerismond, the lawful king, now living as an outlaw in the Forest of the Ardennes. Saladyne bribed the champion to kill Rosader, whom he persuaded to enter the lists against him. Rosader saw the champion kill the two brave sons of a franklin, and, fired by their father's composure and Rosalynd's beauty, succeeded in killing his opponent. On returning home he found the gates shut against him by his brother, but was helped by Adam Spencer, an Englishman, an old and trusty servant of his father.

Seeing his courtiers' admiration for Rosalynd, now equally in love with Rosader, Torismond banished her from the Court. Rosalynd courageously defended herself, Alinda joining her protests, until Torismond angrily dismissed her as well. To journey more safely, the taller Rosalynd went disguised as a page, Ganimede, and Alinda as a maiden, Aliena. Reaching the Forest, for two or three days they saw no human creature, and were often in danger from wild beasts. At last they saw two shepherds, Coridon and Montanus, feeding their flocks, playing on their pipes and discussing Montanus' love pains in a long poetical dialogue. Coridon offered them shelter in his own cottage, and his praise of country life so inspired Aliena that she instructed him to buy a farm for her. They lived for some time tending their flocks and happy in exile.

The story now returns to Rosader, whom Saladyne at last seized. With Adam Spencer, he finally escaped to the Forest, where they lost their way. Though fainting, Adam tried to cheer his young master, who rushed away in a last attempt to get food. He came upon the banished Gerismond and his lords eating at a table under some trees, and, on demanding food at the point of his sword, was kindly bidden to eat. But his first thought was to fetch Adam, a consideration that greatly pleased Gerismond, who welcomed him warmly to his band when he heard that Rosader was the son of an old friend.

Torismond, who wanted the lands of Sir John of Bordeaux, arrested Saladyne, on pretext of the wrongs he had done his brother, and in prison Saladyne repented of all his evil deeds. Sent into banishment, he set out to seek his brother. By this time a forester in Gerismond's band, Rosader used to carve verses in Rosalynd's praise on the bark of trees. He was doing this one day when Aliena and Ganimede came across him, and Ganimede 'shooke him out of his dumpes' by teasing questions about his lady. This meeting reawakened all Ganimede's love, and she proposed to do duty for the absent Rosalynd—Ganimede to call Rosader husband, and he to call Ganimede wife, both promising themselves much pleasure from this game.

Saladyne, having also reached the Forest, lay down and fell fast asleep, while a hungry lion couched, watching, beside him. Rosader, passing by, was amazed to find that the sleeper was his brother. Then Saladyne stirred, and Rosader gave the lion a deadly wound with his boar-spear, getting hurt in return. At the noise Saladyne awoke, and thanked his saviour in courteous terms. Greatly surprised, Rosader heard the tale of repentance, and soon the two brothers were on the most loving terms. As Rosader was telling Ganimede and Aliena the story of their reconciliation, a band of ruffians attacked them, meaning to carry off Aliena, and Rosader, alone against odds, was overcome when Saladyne came to their rescue. Aliena and he fell in love at first sight. While Aliena was suffering from love and Ganimede from anxiety for the wounded Rosader, Coridon tried to entertain them with the story of Montanus' hopeless passion for Phoebe, and brought them to watch where she sat on the grass while Montanus sang her a mournful ditty, and Phoebe gave disdainful answers to all his pleas. Ganimede's passionate attack on Phoebe's vanity had the unlooked-for effect of making the shepherdess fall in love on the spot with 'him'. As Aliena and Ganimede returned to their flocks, Saladyne described to them how the name of Rosalynd was never off his brother's lips, and declared his own passion for Aliena.

Still hoping to win Ganimede, Phoebe made Montanus the bearer of a love-letter to him. Deeply impressed by

Montanus' constancy, Ganimede told Phoebe that 'he' could never marry her, and made her declare that if she could stop loving Ganimede she would love her faithful swain. Ganimede next learned that Aliena and Saladyne were to be married on Sunday, and when Rosader lamented that he could not wed Rosalynd the same day, undertook to bring this about by the help of a friend experienced in magic arts.

On Sunday all were making merry when Montanus joined them, dressed in yellow and wearing a willow garland in token of being forsaken. In reply to Gerismond he told the story of his love. Phoebe told hers, and when Gerismond had Ganimede brought before him the youth's features recalled his daughter Rosalynd. This drew out Rosader's story, and Gerismond declared that if Rosalynd were there he would willingly give her to Rosader. Ganimede then withdrew, and, returning dressed as a woman, presented herself in tears to her father. Everything was now clear, and the three weddings —for Phoebe rewarded Montanus—were at once solemnized. In the midst of their rejoicings, Fernandyne, the second son of Sir John of Bordeaux, arrived with the news that the twelve Peers of France had risen to defend Gerismond's rights, and were about to do battle with Torismond. The King and his followers set off at once, Torismond was killed, and Gerismond conducted in triumph to Paris. As soon as peace was restored, he sent for Rosalynd and Alinda, created Rosader heir to the kingdom, restored Saladyne to his father's lands, chose Fernandyne as his chief secretary, and made Montanus Lord over all the Forest, Adam Spencer Captain of the King's Guard, and Coridon Master of Alinda's Flocks.